CORSET CHRONICLES:

TAILS FROM A KEY WEST STRIP CLUB

By
Charles Meier

This book may sound like a book of fiction, but is mostly true. Some of the names, dates, characters and locations may have been changed to protect the innocent from their parents, boyfriends, girlfriends or other family members finding out that they worked at a strip club even if they are over the age of 40. Mrs. Hope-- sorry about outing you early, and Mrs. La Porta, this means you. I have much love for all my Angels.

Acknowledgements

It would be impossible to thank everyone, so here's the short list. I would like to thank my friends and family, and everyone who purchased my first book, <u>Letters from the Sandbox,</u> and liked it enough to tell me about it.

Mike Haskins and Reef Perkins for getting me back into the writing game. This is the second installment for all of you who begged me to write another one. You asked for it; here it is.

To my mother (Mary Meier) for bringing me into this world kicking and screaming, for teaching me right from wrong, always telling me that I could do anything I put my mind to, having absolute faith in me, and swatting my ass when I needed it.

Ken & Mary Burton for adopting me in the later years and becoming my second family helping me with my other trials and tribulations in life.

To Cheryl Blyth & Caren Denke and Mama Cass for proofing my work and fixing my screw ups misspellings, punctuations, and random capitalizations.

To my Jedi DJ's, Bill Hoebiee, and Rocko who instructed me in the fine arts of verbal diarrhea, and for giving me my strip club voice.

To all the girls I've loved before, the staff and crew at the club; you know who you are. Without you all, none of these adventures would ever have happened. I am so glad I came along for the ride.

To my Rock Star Bartender Staff: Hope, Suzy Q, Brenda la Pourta, Little Mrs. Rebecca, Trudy, & Carry, You all trained me up, kept me out of the shit, out of the weeds, and in the business. Together we rocked that place and made it the best little adult club on the planet. I still have the numbers to prove it.

My security staff: Jason, Grumpy Dave, Jeff, Big Kevin, and Big Gene, for having my back. It was my honor to work with all of you.

To all the ladies who came across the stage while I was managing. Every last one of you taught me something, and I had a great time being at least a little part of your lives.

Lastly, to my wife Dallas, you are my Angel and the greatest love of my life. Thanks for bringing me back from the brink of death, taking care of a one legged old war horse, and being with me every day. You were the brains behind the club scene and every other adventure we have gotten into. I'm looking forward to the next 40 years, babe.

Just something to get you started.

Contents

Acknowledgements
There's Nothing like Listening to a Drunk
The Beginning
Key West Where the Weird Turn Pro
How Did I Get Myself into This
What's it Like Managing a Strip Club
Let's Take a Test
The Ten Commandments of Stripping
Most Common Questions People Ask
Two Types of Strippers
All Types of Customers
I Love You Hank—Fuck You Hank
Boner Ballroom
Vaseline Boy
Attack of the Man Head
Champagne Room OBGYN
Back Alley Orgy
Attack of the Wolf-Pussy
Drink & Drown
Dude I Lost My Teeth
Friends Behaving Badly
Tangerine Sized Testicle
My Friend Monster
I Think I Want to Take it in the Ass.
Sphincter Flexing at the British Boys
Quotes from the Dali Llama
Fantasy Fest
Cock Sock Guy
Love Notes
Tasers/Stun-Guns/Buttholes & Beavers
Tactical Tasering Events
Dave and the Surrender
Dealing with Democrats
Full Vaginal TASING
Tanners Nut TASING

Dick Waving Gone Wild
Karma is a Motherfucker
The Birth of a Five Hour Energy Drink
Door Kicker
Amateurs and Fat Girls
Drunk of the Evening Catching Her Hair on Fire
Switching Teams
TASER Tony
Trifecta of Stupid
Witty Banter with Drunks
Kung Fu Carrot Top
Posers, Wanna-B's & Secret Squirrels
Tattooed Sasquatch
On an Island Where Everybody is Somebody
Countrified Ass Whooping
Spring is in the Air
Memorable Spring Break Moment
Match Boy
Grape Ape
Viking Horn
Strange Shit Dancers Say—Bubbles' Sayings
Boot Licking Piss Drinking Good Time
Dancing with a Dead Guy
Panty Sniffers & Piss drinkers
Operation golden flow
Butt Sex
Super V
Poopie Pants
Bubbles Saying
I've Lost My Vagina.
Rantings of a Mad Stripper

There's Nothing Like Listening to a Drunk Reminiscing

By Tortuga Jack Hacket

There's nothing like listening to a drunk
reminiscing about some yesterday brought to now.

Its O so amazing, the fiction, the phrasing the
clarity while giving an account.

A local history you'll never get to read, for only
seven were present to witness the deed.

All are now gone with exception of one, whom
will seldom tell the tale though he will tell it well.

And there's nothing like listening to a drunk
reminiscing about some yesterday brought to now.

The Beginning

In the beginning God was bored. So, being the all knowing, all seeing Omni-present Alpha and Omega type of dude that he is, he decided to spice shit up a bit. He gave man dominion over the earth and gave woman a vagina; which of course, is the power to rule the world?

Boys this is to let you know that we've been set up. We were fucked from the word go. At the start of our lives we spend nine months trying to get out, and the rest of our lives trying to get back in.

This book is about the trials, and tribulations, action packed alcohol and drug induced adventures and total weirdness in general that happens to the employees, managers, and patrons, who have ventured into a certain little strip club located on Duval Street at the geographical end of the continental United States; just 90 miles from the coast of Cuba.

Welcome to the island.

Key West is Where the Weird Turn Pro

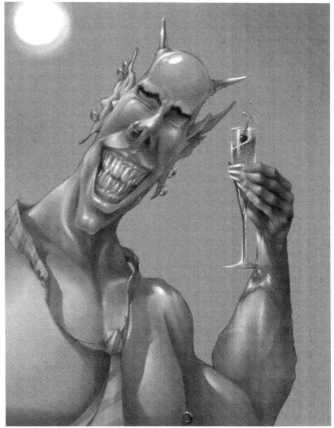

Art by Franklin Rose

Welcome to Key West, one of the oldest cities in Florida. This little outpost consumes more alcohol per capita than any other city in the United States; and with more churches per-capita than any other city in the U.S. We are closer to a communist country than we are to any shopping mall on the main land. We are an Island comprised of sinners and saints.

As the saying goes, Key West is an island where the weird turn pro, drinking is considered an Olympic sport, and bad habits become a career choice. People come on vacation, and leave on probation. Sometimes if the island wants you, you don't leave at all. When the island is tired of you, you will know it, because it will have chewed you up, spit you out, used you like a sun burnt, dick whipped whore, wiped its ass on your cleanest sheets, ripped out your liver and thrown it in the gutter by your bloating corpse just to be spiteful.

If you live in the keys, there are three things to do here.
(1) Drink
(2) S.C.U.B.A dive
(3) Fish.

Everything else revolves around those three industries. And I'm telling you if you are not into any of those things, you may have come to the wrong place. What do you do on an island if you don't like to drink, scuba dive or fish? Boom! The hospitality industry is born. If you arrived here, and have fallen in love with the island and don't want to leave, be prepared to work three jobs to maintain your status as a local. But, the island does give back.

As you change the latitude, you'll notice that there is a definite change in the attitude. The weather is nice with the exception of the occasional nasty hurricane. But on the sunny side, you don't have to worry about freezing, the scenery is great, and you can get into any five star restaurant wearing flip flops and a tank tops.

On this island it's normal for millionaires walk down Duval Street looking likes bums. If you're looking for status or to be recognized, you've come to the wrong place. Turn your ass around and head back to Miami. South Beach is waiting for you.

This is an island where somebody's come to be nobody, and everybody is just fine with that.

I believe that most of the stories in this book you will find hard to believe. Hell, I lived them and as I'm writing this, I still find them hard to believe. But if you live here or have ever lived here, you will understand it's just everyday normal life in Key West.

How Did I Get Myself into This

Well, that's a good question. In my opinion I have had a very blessed life. My resume is long, drawn-out, and unbelievable at best. I started my career as A US Naval Combat Search and Rescue Swimmer/Aircrew men. As a Fireman, and a Cop, I served on SWAT & Dive teams for Monroe County. I lived and worked overseas as a security contractor. I've been blown up six times (three in the same day) and limped away with the help of a real good friend to tell that story too. Look it up. Letters From the Sandbox.

I have been shot at and missed, shit at and hit, knocked down, dragged out of places I can't even remember, beat up, blown up, and stabbed. I'm missing a leg and have broke more bones then I care to reflect upon, grew some back and cut the rest off.

I've been a Bouncer, an Announcer, a DJ and the General Manager of one of the best strip clubs on the planet. I've M.C.'d, Wet T-shirt contests that had nothing to do with wet T-shirts. I've made guys wear dildo helmets in front of hundreds of people on stage. I'm a boat Captain, a pilot, a minister, a motivational speaker, a sky diver, and a S.C.U.B.A diver. I've been on more adventures then most people dream of, and I'm still living that dream.

I love women! All kinds of woman! I'm not sure that I have a particular type. I like big women, small women, short and tall woman. The only prerequisite is they have to have a sense of humor and a personality. Because you can put lipstick on a pig and take her to prom but you will find that a personality and a great sense of humor will get you a lot further in life, once you realize that none of us are actually going to make it out of this world alive.

I enjoy everything about women. If I had to describe myself in the liking women department, I would say I'm kind of like Hugh Heffner without the pipe, the robe, the millions, the mansion and the income from the magazine to support it all.

If I had Hef's money, I would burn all mine. I guess more importantly as the song goes, "I like my woman a bit on the trashy side." untamed if you will. So running a strip club seems like a perfect fit. (except for the jealous wives part, but that my friends is a whole different story.)

To start this out, I'll have to take you way back to my Navy days. There I was, a little 18-21 year old boy. I had just joined the Navy and was living pay check to paycheck like every other enlisted E-nothing, sucking down Raman noodles, and beanie weenie's and still attending what, at the time, some of my oldest and dearest friends (Nix, Donnie, Dave, Tim, Andy, and Al) referred to as our weekly ritual upper chest night, or titty bar Thursday's at our favorite location, and watering hole. It was a strip club called Sammy's in Pensacola, Fl. and, of course, a few of the other adult night clubs in the area.

Sammy's, at the time, was the home of some of the hottest women on the Gulf Coast, and to a group of young Navy men such as ourselves, who were obviously out to save the world, one stripper at a time. This place was the geographical center of the Universe. The women were hot, the beer was cold, the nipples were always perky. The place was dark and air conditioned, and there was always an endless supply of really hot sexy women (bartenders, waitresses, and dancers) to stroke our oh so fragile ego's—telling us how good looking we were and relieving our wallets of the last of our previous paychecks one lap dance at a time. Oh, and the hangover one would receive from a night of drunken debauchery caused by countless Miller Lights and shots of Jose' Cuervo, that fine Mexican tequila, was tolerable the next day; or, almost tolerable. It could have just been because we were all younger and more tolerant of almost drinking ourselves to death the night before.

This of course brings us to the reason we picked Thursday's as our night to venture out into the world and whore around. It was due to Navy payday usually being on Friday. We could arrive, drink like a fish, spend what was left in the bank account and by Friday morning we would still have a little money to survive on for the next 2 weeks. See, it's a win/win in the business world.

Hell, I dropped so much money in that place the establishment gave me my own bar stool. Seriously! I had my name on it and everything. And if that isn't enough I'll tell you I put a down payment on my first future X-wife. No high school sweetheart for me. I just pulled her sweet ass right out of the club, right off the main stage.

Prior to getting into this book I want to make it perfectly clear to the reader that in no way do I want to portray the wrong ideas, or promote common stereotypes that the women in this industry are all whores, idiots, or just plain stupid. As a matter of fact, nothing could be further from the truth. During my years of experience in this business I have met some of the smartest women that I have ever had the privilege to know and I'm still married to one of them. But, I will admit that most of the ranting and writings are not about the smart ones. That would probably be a pretty dull story now, wouldn't it?

What's it like Managing a Strip Club From the Outside Looking In

The actuality is that the illusion is always better than the reality. What the customer sees is simple. Me standing around with several very gorgeous naked women near me at all times. These women are doing any number of things, whispering in my ear, stroking my hair, handing me money and seemingly hanging on my every word. All the while, the music is thumping, bumping, and the base is pumping. The girls are jumping on the stage, swinging on the poles, hanging from the ceilings, gyrating, in front of the customers, feeding them shots and grinding out dances 20 bucks at a time. The bartenders are slinging the drinks like there is no tomorrow, and the world as you know it is Happy, Happy, Happy.

What guy wouldn't want a fantasy like that?

Well my friend's this reality is a fallacy. Welcome to Oz, or our island of misfit toys. Now if you want the truth, all you have to do is pull back the curtains and look for the conductor of this crazy train. You don't have to look too hard. I'm right here hiding in plain sight.

I would always say to people who walked up and attempted to inform me I was the luckiest guy on earth, or I had it made, "You have a wife or girl friend? Is she a pain in the ass sometime?" Now multiply that by 30 or 40 every night, add that most of them are drinking and getting drunk. Some are on drugs, a couple of them are certifiably fucking crazy, half of them are on the rag, and 90% of them are bitching about something that one of their coworkers may or may not be doing. We have not even got to the boyfriends, girlfriends, X's, stalkers, pimps, drug dealers, and unruly customers yet.

Think you could handle that?

Managing the ego's and menstrual cycles of 40 women is like herding cats or nailing Jell-O to a tree—and that, my friends, is on an easy day. I get to orchestrate the controlled chaos that happens between these two stages, four bartenders, three security staff, a DJ, and 30 to 40 strippers, and an unknown number of customers this evening alone. But you don't need to know any of that. Grab your wallet, get out of the cheap seat, sit down in the erection section and start living that fantasy one dollar at a time.

Let's Take a Test

The Rational and Irrational Questionnaire for an Exotic Dancer in Key West

1. **What do you do when you hear your name called for standby for your stage set?**

   (a) Go on break and smoke a joint.
   (b) Go to the bar and start doing shots.
   (c) Go play your music and get ready for stage.
   (d) Go to the dressing room and start a fight.

2. **How do you handle another dancer that is pissing you off?**

   (a) Throw her make up in the trash.
   (b) Write dirty messages about her on the dressing room mirror using her lipstick.
   (c) Discuss it with the manager and let him handle it.
   (d) Go tell the bitch how you feel and if she gets mouthy slap that whore for being disrespectful.

3. When should you pay your house/floor fee?

(a) After you have had $30-$50 dollars worth of drinks.
(b) After being asked 10 times by management.
(c) When you come in.
(d) Never, maybe if you're quiet the manager will forget about you.

4. What should you do when a customer refuses to pay for a lap dance?

(a) Assault him with a 6" inch stiletto spiked shoe and call the police.
(b) Call for security and let them deal with it.
(c) Nothing House rules state get the money prior to your dance.
(d) Nothing according to the drunk customer, you never gave him a lap dance.

5. How should you handle a rude customer?

(a) Say nothing. Go to the dressing room, drink five shots and cry.
(b) Slap them, and make up an elaborate story about how he touched your pussy.
(c) Tell security and let them handle it.
(d) Accidently spill their drink in their lap.

6. If you are scheduled to work at 7:00p.m., what time should you show up for work?

(a) 10:30, "Hell I'll pay the late fee."
(b) 8:30
(c) 6:45
(d) Fuck it. You have better things to do with you time.

7. **When you miss your stage set who is to blame?**

   (a) The Dj
   (b) The bartender, but you just had to have that drink.
   (c) You
   (d) The customer/drug dealer that you're still
       trying to get your money or drugs from.

8. **If lap dances are $20.00 what should you charge?**

   (a) That depends on how hot they are and what exactly
       it is that they want to do.
   (b) Depends on how drunk the customer is.
   (c) $20.00 bucks. No exceptions.
   (d) Fuck it, it's a slow night, I'll let you fondle me
       for a $10 spot.

9. **What should you do if any of your belongings go
   missing?**

   (a) Immediately go through all the other girls' things
       because one of these fucking bitches took my shit.
   (b) Pitch a Bitch Fit and start accusing all the girls you
       don't like of stealing your stuff.
   (c) Tell the manager and let him handle it,
       steal what was taken from you from one of the
       other girls.

10. **When should you mind your own business and not Interrupt your coworkers?**

(a) When a manager or security is dealing with a customer.
(b) When a bartender is dealing with a customer.
(c) When another dancer is talking with a customer.
(d) When the waitress is dealing with a customer.
(e) All of the above, your only business is getting naked and collecting the money.

11. **You have been told by management that you should not drink, you should:**

(a) Heed his words.
(b) Mix pain pills with your cocktail of choice to help intensify the buzz.
(c) Why stop you're going to walk on the tab anyway.
(d) You don't need to stop, you're doing enough blow to balance yourself out. You'll be fine.

Please keep in mind all of these questions and answers came from actual events

If you answered **C** for most of the answers you would make a lot of money in this career. If you failed miserably don't worry you can still be a dancer.

The Ten Commandments of Stripping

As with every profession or job come the rules. If you should attempt employment at a Booby Barn, Poontang Pavilion, Pussy Palace, or the local Hard on Hacienda, here are my top 10 rules or commandments on running a strip club. I have found in life, it's the little shit that makes life easier. I handed out these rules to all employees prior to them working for me, and posted them in the dressing room for all to see, just to verify that we were all on the same sheet of music.

(1) <u>Strippers Have a Shelf Life:</u> There is a direct correlation with how you normally act, the amount of drugs/alcohol that you inject, ingest, or inhale, the lifestyle that you choose, and the decisions that you make. Act accordingly.

(2) <u>Stripping is a Full Contact Beauty Contest and the New Models are Arriving Daily:</u> If you're not taking care of yourself, i.e. working out, tanning, primping, staying healthy, body maintenance, and landscaping. Your shelf life will be reduced greatly.

(3) <u>Grooming Standards:</u> The days of the 1970's safari beaver are over. It's now 2010. If you bend over and it looks like a service monkey is attempting to escape from your asshole you're doing something wrong. Shave, wax, pluck or do whatever it takes. Just fix the problem!

(4) <u>Significant Others:</u> Husbands, boyfriends, girlfriends, X's, pimps, and all other wannabe managerial types are not allowed in the club while you're working. I am the only manager that you need while you're here at this club.

(5) <u>Get the Money Up Front $$$:</u> Stripping is your business. If you are not in the Business to Make Money, why the Hell are you here wasting time? There are other industries that

you may want to try, K-Mart, Wall-Mart, or other fine stores; perhaps the food service industry, Checkers, McDonalds, Burger King, or maybe Dions, the local chicken joint down the street. If you can't cut it here, practice the Mantras: "Do you want fries with that?" or, "Paper or plastic?" These options give you a paycheck, and, you don't have to worry about collecting your money. They also give you a schedule. If you make me get the money for you, I'll be keeping a portion of it for my trouble.

(6) No Penetration what-so-ever: No Kissing, No Fucking, No Sucking, and No Hand jobs on yourself or the customer. These are things prostitutes do for money. Professional strippers sell illusions of availability fantasies and dreams (but inconveniently they are never available).
There are three things we can provide for our customers, Drunk, Horny, and Broke in that order!

(7) Honest Assessments/Managerial Decisions: I'm the guy who hears what the customers say after you leave, as you walk by or get off the stage. When It gets bad enough, or starts costing the Club or other girls' money, I'll tell you. If you think that you are fat, smell bad, or look like a man you probably do. If you want to remove all doubts or need clarification, just ask me.

(8) Scheduling: Strippers do not have schedules. You are all contractors and pay to work here. I understand that there are just some days that you don't feel like grinding cock or dealing with customers. Therefore, you have the luxury of working when and if you want to. But, you have to be here on time for shift, and you have to bring your house fee with you. If you're late, pay the fine. No sniveling.

(9) Communication: If you are having an issue or problem, my suggestion would be use your big girl voice, and try talking to the DJ's, managers, or bartenders about it.

English is the preferred language. If you can't speak English learn or bring an interpreter with you.

Note: There are times that the batteries are dead in our crystal balls and our mind reading capabilities are hindered. If you do not like the music the DJ plays, remove that song from your play list or add a different one.

(10) Fighting: We DO NOT fight amongst each other here. If you can't act like a lady this may not be the job for you. If I cannot find out who the primary aggressor is, (that means who started the shit storm) I am now forced to deal with both parties will be fired/suspended and or fined heavily for their indiscretions.

The Most Common Questions People Ask

The questions run the gambit. I have heard almost everything and usually had a pretty good explanation for most. The next couple of pages should clear up the common questions for the un-initiated.

Usually somewhere near the top of the list was something like, "How much do these girls make a night?"

That my friend always depends on a shit load of variables; is the girl a hustler, or is she a barfly? The Hustler uses the shotgun approach. She will go out and ask every customer in the bar for a dance. Like a terminator, she is there to get the money, even if it's one dollar at a time. The Barfly will sit at the bar sipping on one drink at a time until one lucky customer drops a ball and comes to talk to her or she targets one lucky guy and he's it for the evening.

What season is it? Is there a holiday, big event or festival in town? A lot of girls travel the circuit. Meaning they go from town to town, event or show. Whatever brings the customers and where-ever the wind blows them.

The answer to the question—I have seen girls walk out with $15 grand from one guy one night, and I have had girls who couldn't pay house after the evening was over. It depends on the girl and the night.

It's a combination of sales 101, supply and demand and basic economics. If you got something someone wants, they will pay for it. Lap dances are $20 bucks for a three minute set, or $400 dollars an hour, if you break it down to an hourly wage. Did I just get your attention?

The stage sets are one dollar or two at a time from every ass in the seat. So if you have ten people at the stage you could probably average a minimum of $20 bucks for a three minute song. And remember, we have two sets. Oh excuse, me four sets. There's a back stage that the dancer gets to do it again. But of course that depends on the customers.

There are times it's a real roller coaster for the ladies. The only thing you can count on is the bar will make its money. It will be dark and smoky, the music will be loud, the beer will be cold and you will have competition.

There are Two Types of Strippers

I would say the number one thing that I used to hear from customers and people in general, was this question, "What kind of girl does this for a living?" Of course, whore, slut, prostitute, drug addict, were just a few of the general stereotypes that run through one's mind and then so easily roll off the tongue. In the old days a job like this was hidden from the general public and you didn't dare tell anyone what you did for a living.

The second most common question is, "Why would a woman want to do this type of job?"

Simple answer is because you are your own boss; cash money pays the bills in the most efficient manner. You can make your own schedule, take vacations when you want, and it gives you the most time off work so that they are still able to spend precious time with their families, work on continuing education, pay the rent, buy a house, or houses, car or cars, a business, go on vacations or whatever else they want to do. Of course as with anything else, you have the extreme other end of the spectrum, too. With a job like this you can support one hell of a drug habit. Thank God we have jumped forward more into the mainstream and I guess we can credit the women for this. They have realized that strippers have kick ass bodies, most of them are in awesome shape, and as mentioned, they have their bills paid, nice cars, and plenty of time off. And it's directly because of what they do. But stripping isn't easy. To do a job like this for any length of time, you have to work.

I'll say it now and you'll hear it over and over again throughout this book; stripping is a full contact beauty contest with a shelf life.

The older you get the better you used to be. That goes with anything. My friends, that is just the way it is, and there is nothing that any of us can do about it.

I am happy to say that it seems these days everybody wants to be a stripper. Just take a look at pole dance classes out in public, fat girls, thin girls, and working moms all taking up the fine art of working the pole. Something that used to be really taboo—no self-respecting woman would be caught on a pole. For some reason it is now socially acceptable to be a stripper.

The simple truth is almost anyone can be a stripper. Students, housewives, moms, the only thing you really need in this industry is a vagina, and the ability to walk on a stage strip buck naked in front of fifty to a hundred people you have never seen before (maybe some that you have), and take their money one dollar at a time. Presto, you have an instant revenue stream anyplace on the planet. Any state, city, town or country you will find someplace where someone wants to look at a naked woman.

Warning: Dancing is a limited time offer with a shelf life. As the saying goes, beauty is skin deep, personality goes a long way, but ugly is to the bone.

The goal is get in, get the money, have a backup plan, and get the hell out alive.

The answer to the original question of what kind of woman dances is, all kinds from all different walks of life. In one way I guess it's almost the oldest profession in the books.

Now we flash forward and jump into the new age where stripping is no longer taboo.

The girl who does this for a living can be broken down into two different types:

.

(1) Girls who strip for a living: They use their money wisely, pay the bills, pay for college, set up their future business, and buy houses or property. You know, set themselves up for their future and live comfortably ever after. They understand that there is a shelf life.

(2) Girls who strip for a lifestyle. These ladies just live the rock star lifestyle. They really burn the candle at both ends. Sex, drugs, and rock & roll in abundance. Sometimes they burn out, most of the time they just fade away.

The ladies in this business come from every background imaginable; they have everybody style you would fantasize about, and numerous types of personalities. Some girls even have multiple personalities. Everything from the shy girl next door type, to the outlandish blow your mind dominatrix type. They also come from varied and diverse educational backgrounds. I have had girls work for me who were real live rocket scientists, lawyers, psychologists, teachers, college students, and single moms, and one of them may be the girl sitting next to you right now. All of them, just making a living, using what God and maybe a plastic surgeon or two have given them, and paid for it one lap dance at a time.

Of course I have had the luxury of dealing with the bottom of the barrel hookers, crack heads, and straight up hoe's, too.

This book contains a lot of stories about them and most seem outlandish and absurd. In no way should this writing generalize the people in the industry. But be warned it is going to be a shit show.

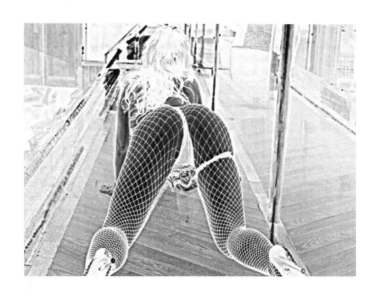

All Types of Customers:
Gawkers, Goobers, Shmoooooooows, Fetish Guys, and Freaks

Damn near everybody has walked through the doors, down the dimly lit halls, passed the private dance rooms and landed a seat at the bar or in the front row of the boner ball room.

My clientele list is long and covers the gambit of society. Admirals to assholes, pastors, preachers, clerks, city councilmen, cops, criminals, deviants, drug dealers, pimps, prostitutes, ministers, motivational speakers, rock stars, wrestlers, race drivers, movie stars, midgets, and soccer moms.

I'm about to break you in to a little dancer code if you will. These terms of endearment came about from the dancers themselves. When translated the terms explain the amount of money that a dancer may get from a customer at any given time.

Gawkers: The people that just come in don't tip, don't drink, take up valuable space and hold up the wall. They act like they are too good to be in the place but stay to stare at the process anyway.

Interestingly enough if you get a female gawker who just looks appalled to be in the place, she will usually be an above average or pretty girl in the looks department. She is used to getting all the attention, all the time, and due to her current location—surrounded by a lot of lovely naked ladies—has seemingly dropped her on the desirability scale, so she is getting none of her usual attention. As a M.C., D.J. or Manager I have found that you can use that against her.

Massage her fragile ego, hand her a shot of liquid courage, and tell her that she would look good on stage. BOOM!!!! You have changed a Gawker to an amateur. A winning game plan for everyone, boy friend gets a shot at a fantasy, the girl gets to have all of her seemingly lost attention back, and the crowd love amateurs.

Goobers: A repeat regular, the monthly or weekly customer who has limited resources, and usually only a couple of zeros in his bank account. A Goober actually thinks that he is courting the dancer. The dancer will give them the light girlfriend experience, i.e. hand holding, sitting at the table talking, and then of course finish with a very meaningful lap dance, eye contact and everything until she has successfully removed the last dollar from his wallet, bank account, or cab fare home.

The dancer would want the Goober to feel as if he/she is really important and that she really cares.

She has to remember a Goobers name, birthday, and certain events in his or her life; especially when his or her pay day is.

$$SHMOOOOOOOOOOOOOOOOOOOw's$$ Also Known as Whale: this person has unlimited zeros in the bank account. Obviously you can get a lot more out of them than the Goober.

A SHMOOOOOOOOOw is usually somewhere high up in the business world, he owns a company, or companies. He is always traveling and is seeking companionship, an arm piece, someone to take to dinner or business meetings or the ultimate girl friend experience. The Shmooooo package usually comes standard with unlimited shopping trips, houses, vacations, to where-ever, whenever, and the girl's bills being paid. He or she is going to write it off as a business expense anyway.

Just for clarification, sex does not have to be involved in this type of relationship. Amusingly enough the longer sex is not involved the more money the girl can get out of a Shmooooooooo; houses, cars, weekly or monthly income; all this comes standard just to be available at the beckoned call of a $$Schmoooooooow$$.

To hook a Shmoooooo you have to bring your A game. A $$Shmoooooooow$$ wants her to remember him immediately; his birthday, his wife, his kids, and sometimes even his pet's names. She will know his favorite food, favorite team, and favorite hobby. She has to be in shape, fun, educated, spontaneous, adventurous, up to date on current events, sports, and politics. She is lady in public, a cook in the kitchen, and a whore everywhere else.

A $$Shmoooooow$$ has the ability to save the world one stripper at a time, or maybe he's saving six strippers in six different cities at the same time. Either way he can afford it.

Fetishists & Freaks: An added bonus of ass-hattery, these guys step up the game and sometimes do it for shock value or to test their limitations in the game. They are also an integral part of the extreme club experience. They usually have money and pay well for the experience and the anonymity that comes standard with that practice.

You may be surprised at the income brackets and background of some of these people. The kinkier they are usually means the higher up the food chain they usually are.

Let's start out with guys at the low range of the kink factor. This is someone we refer to as the everyday Joe. Then we move on to the panty sniffer experience. Who don't like a good old whiff of the crotch every now and then? Then we graduate up the ladder with the stocking and shoe fetish guys, and possibly a little nipple clamp action.

Next comes, the real fetish and freak show. The boys who want to be dominated, have a madam or mistress tie them up, slap them around, and kick em in the balls a few times just to start the session off right. Then the mistress gets to tell them exactly what to do and when to do it, drags them around on a leash in the middle of the club on all fours like a dog, pets them on the head then points out when to talk, what to say, and whose shoes to lick during the process.

Or you can have the princess pretty show pony experience. What is that you may ask?

Allow me to enlighten you on this lovely experience. One of the girls had a very high end customer; I believe that he was called Admiral or General in real life. And he loved this service which included a mask, a bit and bridle, a saddle and a really large horse hair butt plug that resembled a tail sticking out of his ass while she was riding him around the room, buck naked beating him like a jockey on race day. Of course this didn't happen in the club. Due to the person involved it was an out call situation, as one might expect, it was taken to a more secure location.

I don't judge. Shots of warm piss and ball sack bondage for everybody. As long as you are not hurting anybody else, you are not a pedophile, and pay your tab at the end of the evening you're good to go.

Oh, there are a couple of people that I didn't add; drug dealers, pimps, dancer's boyfriends, and hangers on. These dipshits are most closely akin to the Gawkers, except not as useful. All are self explanatory and as a manager a direct pain in the ass.

I Love You Hank—Fuck You Hank!

Flash back to one of the first times that is permanently etched in my mind. The location was again that quaint little club called Sammy's. This is where I spent my 21st birthday, not to mention most of my shore duty enlistment while stationed in Pensacola Fl. At the time, in my logical thinking mind, there was no better place to spend my 21st birthday then in a strip club surrounded by a group of my best friends, to help celebrate this milestone in my life.

The evening started out great. Girls were hot; the beer was cold and flowed freely from the kegs, and bottles. Being in the Navy, drinking was elevated from a simple rite of passage, to an Olympic fucking sport.

It was on this day, my 21st birthday that I was truly introduced to my new found friends Jack Daniels and Jose' Cuervo. So after drinking the libations of love and of course killing a few hundred thousand brain cells in the process, the most memorable part of that evening commenced.

My fiends took up a collection to get my ass up on stage during the world famous Sammy's roll call. Hoisted to the heavens, there I was, half cocked, all jacked, ready, and ready to rock. I was surrounded by 20 or so beautiful women, doing a birthday dance for sweet little ol' me. Yep, I was on top of the world, or at least on top of the stage at Sammy's, feeling like a king and getting my friends monies worth, too; thinking, "Ahhh! It's great to be 21. I should do this shit every day."

After the song was over, I was expeditiously removed from the stage and hoisted back down into the crowd with my buddies and the rest of the common folks again.

This would have been fine with one exception. Once you're up there, you're always trying to get back to Shangri-la. Added to this particular situation was the person they replaced me with, none other than Hank Williams Jr., the world famous country music star.

Now, being a Texas boy, having grown up in Fredericksburg, Texas, I love me some Hank Williams Jr. I grew up listening to Hank. He was everywhere, BBQ's, birthday parties, festivities, and town fairs. Hell, my sister had an old 60's Valiant with an eight track player in the glove box, and Hank was on the top of that list too.

So, somewhere in my drunken, convoluted state of mind, I felt like Hank and I knew each other. But, it would seem, that my brain cells were obviously hindered by high volumes of fermented alcoholic beverages and were having issues negotiating logical thinking. Hence the reason, that I couldn't figure out any logical reason why I was not up on that stage basking in the glory of half naked women right alongside of Mr. Hank Williams Jr.

Against the better judgment of my not so intoxicated friends I apparently wanted to profess my love and adoration personally to Hank while he was on the stage. Somehow I got away from my buddies: Nix, AL, Donnie, Andy, Dave and Tim. I crawled onto the stage and started screaming at Hank, proclaiming my love for him, and his songs. All this while he was surrounded by the same beautiful women that I previously had dancing and prancing around me, and showering me with attention. What the hell? I want more attention. I want the attention that Hank is getting.

I figured that Hank was a reasonable man, I listened to him all my life; I understood his songs, we connected, why the hell wouldn't he want to share the stage with a fan like me, or at least that's what I thought in my 21 year old mind.

So, I stumbled toward him, and apparently, I didn't see, and/or failed to recognize that Hank Williams has about a size 12" pointed ass toe cowboy boot, which he immediately firmly planted right in the front of my face.

It was at this point that I received, what I call, an education. Not a traditional form of education, but one that uses what I affectionately call, "<u>Boot to the fucking head therapy</u>." You may have heard about this. Some people call this the school of hard knocks. I will tell you that this manner of education is very effective.

You see, it has become apparent to me that humans, including myself, have a problem learning lessons in life, and I now realize that since the beginning of time everything has a had price.

Some people are easy studies, and can learn from example, or by listening to others' stories. While some, like myself take a little more persuasion or time to learn. Add to this equation, that a lesson is not a lesson, until a couple of things happen:
(1) a lesson will cause you pain or loss of money, or
(2) a true lesson will cost you both. I my friends, am the beneficiary of the later. In my drunken haze, it would seem that at light speed at least two, out of the three of my still functioning brain cells had smashed together and I came to the realization that Hank did not share the same feelings that I had.

Now here I am, falling off a three foot elevated stage back into the arms of my friends (Nix, Donnie, Andy, and Dave) screaming obscenities, and ranting about how much I hate fucking, bearded ass, mirrored sunglass having, redneck, boot wearing Hank mother fucking, Williams Jr.

Who the fuck was he to kick me in the face, smash my nose cause the blood to run down my shirt, embarrass the ass off of me and provide me with a formal education regarding strip club etiquette?

I guess I can proudly say I was educated by none other then the professor of hard knocks, author/singer/song writer of Why Do You Drink, Hank Williams Jr. That's who... Well at least I'm man enough to admit I got myself a well deserved countrified ass whooping by Hank.

Shortly after my ass was finished hitting the deck of the bar, security strongly urged our departure from the premises. I was ushered kicking and screaming to an already waiting vehicle which prevented my detainment and arrest by a local constable for something like drunk and disorderly conduct, Herky & jerky with intent to gawk, Otherwise known as public intoxication or any number of other laws that are written in the Florida statutes.

That little episode happened on April 18th 1991. I told you I put a down payment on a future X wife. That was also the evening that began that well rounded event. Let the record show I ended up fucking around, hooking up, living with and marrying that woman. All I can say is that she was a real spit fire, a big tittied, Irish Mexican hottie from Indiana and crazy as a shit house rat. I strapped in and held on for the ride and the veil was lifted. At that moment, I went from being a customer to someone with stock in the company.

My Navy career sent me to The Keys, the brand new X wife tagged along for some reason and started working the club scene in the southernmost city and I got a part time security job at one of the biggest clubs in Key West. That's not saying much for a 2 x 4 mile island. Kirby started working on the adult entertainment side for a woman named Onnie who just happened to be the House Mom for the place. For some unknown reason Onnie took a liking to me. She brought me into the strip club to do security. At the time I wasn't sure if it was to keep the customers in line or to keep the girls away from her. Either way, I learned a lot about communication with strippers from her. Since then for whatever reason, I have in some form or another been involved in the business end of strip clubs, naked women and beer joints ever since. Over the years, I have worked as a Bouncer, Announcer, DJ, and General Manager of some of the finest adult entertainment facilities in the southern most end of the continental United States.

You know what they say if you're going to have a job, pick something that you have fun doing because then it's less like work. I have to agree. Especially when the naked women are giving you money to stand there and watch them do the voodoo they do, do so well.

Welcome to the Boner Ballroom.

Come one, come all, to the pussy palladium, the pun tang pavilion, the kooter castle, hooter hacienda, hard on hotel, hair care, tire center, and butt bongo fiesta. We will lubricate you with libations, fill your head with fantasies, and liberate your wallet. We take cash, credit and coins of the realm. So gentlemen step right up, sit down, strap in, and hold on. On tonight's menu we have everything that you could want, need, or love. You like pussy? We got all kinds of pussy: big pussy, small pussy, hairy pussy, and bald pussy. Our girls come in all shapes and sizes—they are long, lean, sexy and mean, or short stout and will throw your ass about. I have everything from runway models to body builders, from 18 to 80, blind, cripple and crazy. It's like an all you can eat buffet of puss-waaa-yeaaaaaa! If we don't have the kind of pussy you're looking for, you, my friend, are not looking for pussy. But congratulations, you've made it to Key West, right town—wrong end of the street.

If you're in the mood for a nice cock meat sandwich, with a side of foreskin or maybe some good ol fashioned balls across the chin, I can also point you in the right direction. You can hang out with your wang out and party with the lady boys at the other end of the island. Just keep on walking to the 800 block of Duvall, and you too will be in heaven.

Now, if you have decided that you're in the right place and you have a shitload of bucks burning a hole in your pocket, sit back, relax, and enjoy the show. Were about to take off so, sit down, strap in, and hold on because here we go.

Ladies & Gentlemen, boys & girls, Kids of all ages come one, come all. Welcome to daddy day care. We have 20 beautiful women, two ugly ones, a fat one, a pregnant one, and one that used to be a man. But you have to figure that one out for yourself. I have a lactating lady who will fill a shot glass with blue breast milk for $20, and for $50 she'll squirt your buddies in the face when she comes on stage. I have a female body builder with a clit bigger than your thumb, and a chick that lights her nipples on fire, a girl with six piercings in her pussy, and another that does an amazing act that you will have to see up close and personal like. I'll give you a hint it, involves a pearl necklace, a blanket and a bottle of lotion.

Vaseline Boy

This event happened during my first tour in the adult industry under the guidance and mentorship of a woman named Onnie who was my first boss, the house mom and head madam of the boner ballroom. The shift started out like most other days, and then in walked this customer. He was a white boy, average height, and average weight, wearing a black Stetson cowboy hat, T-shirt, cut off blue jean shorts and boots. Everything seemed to above board so far. He walked up to the bar and ordered a drink, when he pulled out his wallet I noticed that it was packed full of nothing but $20's and $50's.

Then I noticed that the spot that he had been leaning on had a shiny residue to it. At first I didn't think anything of it. I figured he was just hot and a little sweaty. I mean it is Key West, and it's Africa hot here in the summer time. When Onnie went to wipe the bar down the smudge didn't go away it just kind of spread all over the place, because of the the fact he was completely covered in what appeared to be Vaseline.. He left a $20 for a tip so not really a big deal. I watched him as he went to the back of the stage and waited for one of the dancers to arrive. He strategically placed his money in distinct piles of twenties and fifties. Somehow I knew that the first girl on stage was in for a surprise.

When she arrived she didn't notice anything but the piles of cash next to him, and she was going to do whatever it took to get that money. She positioned herself directly in front of him, and I noticed the blanket and bottled lotion come out of her little accessory pack. Then proceeded to go forth with, what is known as a floor show that would blow your mind. She squeezed the bottle and began forcing the dripping lotion out of the end of the bottle and it was now glowing in the black light, running down her breasts, the front of her stomach and when she turned over, the crack of her well rounded ass. She started rubbing it into her skin and was gyrating like a woman lost in the throes of ecstasy.

In my opinion, let's just say the game was on and she should have received a fucking Oscar for her acting capability. She made sure that she had his total undivided attention, and he tipped accordingly.

Apparently this specific customer was what we call in the business one hell of an ass man. The closer her ass got to him, the more money came off the top of the piles. Then, as soon as she removed her panties, let's just say it really got interesting. I watched as Vaseline Boy took in a real deep breath through his nose. He started sniffing up all the sent particles in the air. Then he reached over the stage grabbed her now discarded G string and stuck it to his face as he handed her a hundred dollars. Usually this would have been an issue, but this customer brought money to the equation, and money makes a lot of things all right. Your average cheap G string goes for about $25 bucks. So this girl just rocked a $75 dollar profit on the panties alone and didn't even have to touch the guy. These are the kinky fetish guys that dancers love. Low maintance, they are in the club for one reason, and usually have the money to get their freak on.

Club Note: I have been told that the guys who want to lick shoes are for some reason more prevalent then the panty sniffers.

Getting back to Vaseline Boy. Now he's got a set of panties and is wearing them like a surgical mask. You can see the crotch sucking up to his nostrils every time he takes a breath. Now he's getting all amped up. His chair falls down as he starts humping the air and moving some of the other customers out of the way as he follows our girl stage side as she is making her rounds. He continues his spastic gyrations, pumping and humping as he's handing out $20's and leaving a slime trail all the way down the stage.

At this point Onnie is losing her mind. She is yelling at me to do something, and I ask her what do you want me to do? He's not doing anything wrong, but sucking the scent of pussy out of an old pair of panties, and dry humping the other non-tipping customers out of his way. They seem to be just as amused as I am at the moment, so he's not hurting anyone, and he's tipping the girls, drinking his beer, and is the current source of amusement for everyone else in the bar.

She said, "But look at the mess he's making. Who's going to clean that up?" That's when our boy ran out of room on the stage. He hit the back wall and couldn't move any further down the line. We watched him take his hand and grab a chain that was attached to his belt and disappeared somewhere under his cut off shorts, and give it a ball wrenching, cock tugging jerk. I heard the chain slap against his thigh, and then watched as his skull snap backward, his eyes rolled up in his head, and he collapsed on the floor quivering in the fetal position.

My friends, this was one of those, "What the fuck?" moments. Onnie is once again screaming at me to get him! So I started walking over toward him. I noticed Onnie grab the spray Windex and a bar rag, and begin feverishly attempting to clean the slime trail from the stage area. As I neared him, Vaseline Boy's eyes opened, he stood up, composed himself, and walked back to his original seat at the stage as if nothing happened.

I asked him if everything was ok, and he replied, "Yeah sure, why wouldn't it be?" Oh, no reason, no reason at all.

He looked at Onnie as she was wiping up the smeared mess, grabbed his beer in one hand, and with the other he handed her a petroleum filled fifty dollar bill with a nice shiny frowning picture of President Grant. Then, he asked if he could get a waitress to retrieve him another beer. I asked Onnie, "You still want me to throw him out?"

She looked at the fifty whipped it off with the bar rag then strategically placed it in her bra somewhere and said, "Hell no. He ain't doing anything wrong—why the hell would you want to throw him out?" I laughed and returned to my spot loaded up on more Windex and bar rags and prepped for the next couple of hours of entertainment.

Mrs Onnie

Attack of the Man Head

Man Head. She was a stripper that went way past her prime, but for some reason still made lots of money. In my opinion she looked like the Warner Brothers Frog (hat included). Apparently she went off her medication for bi polar disorder, Epstein Bar virus, mad cow or whatever she had. When I asked why she wasn't taking her medication she stated that she had found religion. Her son had apparently prayed for her and she thought she was cured of her afflictions, or demons.

What she didn't get was that in my perception of a fact based reality, what really happened was that she replaced her medication with alcohol in abundance, and it was making her fucking nuts, and a lot more unstable than normal. I also heard through the coconut telegraph that instead of medication, she and her husband were doing large amounts of cocaine. But in her defense, she told me that she "blessed and prayed over the cocaine prior to doing it, because that's the Christian thing to do, and that makes it all better now, don't it?"

Seriously, you can't make this shit up.

This is the same girl who came in after I fired her for failure to maintain standards (this in laymen's terms just means that her career as a dancer was over because she no longer resembled a woman that I would allow on stage). This, friends, is a big part of the prerequisites for the job. At the very least you have to look like a woman. Or she could not speak English, to communicate effectively with clients, couldn't walk and chew bubble gum at the same time, or lost her personality in a card game. Whatever.

She stated that she had talked to God and that He told her to come back to work for me. I informed her that she must have been confused, because I didn't get that memo.

Then I pointed to the back door, and stated, "You must have misunderstood the message." It would seem to me that she has once again chosen the wrong life path. But sometimes people need to hit rock bottom prior to getting up and crawling out of a hole. Sometimes it doesn't work and they just self destruct or die. That is called natural selection and evolution, a very unfortunate part of the business, but it is reality.

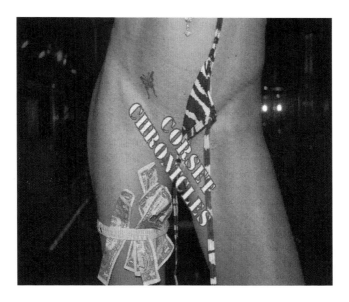

Champaign Room OBGYN

Ok, as everyone knows by now, if you have made it through the book this far, you have already read some weird shit. If you just opened to this page, lucky you, you're going to read some weird shit. So there I am, looking at the video surveillance system...oh, just in case you didn't realize it; there is nothing private about a private dance. In this day and age, all the rooms have cameras in them. Not just for the girls' safety but for the customers, too.

Now back to the story. On this particular evening I was monitoring the video and notice one of my girls who we will call Frenchie, up in the champagne room with a customer, who just happens to be a local doctor, and resident bar fly extraordinaire. Things are going well, or as well as to be expected. At present they are just sitting and talking. Nothing out of the ordinary as of yet; I have seen this a thousands of times. It's his money; he can spend it up here or at the psychologist office. Then I notice Frenchie get up, stand in front of the good doctor, do a little dance, and then turn around, grab her ass, and spread her cheeks wide open. Ok still not too terribly bad, nothing out of the ordinary. I mean, if the customer wants a closer look at the finer parts of the female anatomy, and he paid for the perceived privacy to do so, good for him. Then I see the good doctor take out a pen light, put it in his suck hole as he grabs Frenchie's ass cheeks and jacks them really wide open and dives right in like a mole in a hole looking for the gold. I Ricky-tic my ass up the stairs two hops, a jump, and one skip.

I open the door and look Frenchie in the face as I ask her, "What the Fucks going on?"

To which she responds in a French accent "Oh, This is no problem he's a doctor."

"Yes I know, we've met, but is he a gynecologist and if so, what the fucks e looking for?" I replied.

Gentle readers he has just breached the sacred bonds of **Tip don't touch**. Then the good doctor looks up all bright eyed from staring at the bushy tail of the dancer in front of him, his light dropped out his mouth and hit the floor with a thud, as he asked, "What? Did I do something wrong?" Yeah Dude. I think you did. I broke out in the gospel according the Righteous Reverend Chuck from high atop the pulpit of the Temple of the Hedonist Bull. I singled out the indiscretions of the flock, gave the blessing to the obviously blind, allowed the continued communion and handled the situation.

Ladies and gentlemen, as they say there is NO SEX in the Champaign room. But it would seem some girls will take a free doctor visit when they can get one.

Back Alley Orgy

There are times when you live in the Keys that you think you've seen everything, and then you just know you shouldn't say something that stupid. This was one of those times. It was after a Fantasy Fest, and I was closing out the bar—end of the night stuff, taking out the shit cans, killing the alley lights and rounding the corner.

All of a sudden I hear grunting, moaning, groaning and all manner of other noises that I couldn't identify or understand in the darkness. So to get a better look at what I may be getting into, I shined my flash light in the general direction of the ruckus and found a pile of humanity feverishly humping what I can only describe as a crack hoe.

Amusingly enough these fine fellows just happened to be three guys whom I had removed from the club hours earlier for being cheap fucks and soliciting prostitution. I would guess, by the looks of things, they found something they could afford. The sight was something out of a gangbang movie gone wrong. This girl was, as they say, air tight. Two boys banging her from the backside, one on the bottom the other on her back and her front end was filled up, too. All I saw from the back side was ten toes up, ten toes down, and two little assholes going round and round. As the flashlight shown across the front of her face, the view didn't get any better. When she came up for air, wiped the slobbering drool from her soup cooler while continuing to whack one of the willing participants wiener without missing a stroke, she informed me that she had room for one more.

I had to say, "Where? Sweetheart, looks to me like your dance card is full, and it's definitely not my kind of shindig."

Now, due to lack of attention, one of the pant-less pricks started getting grumpy.

He told me, "If you're not joining the party, you should just move on."

To which I responded, "Bumping nuts with you numbskulls is not my idea of a good time, you fellers are going to get something on your dicks Ajax can't get off. Oh, by the way you should finish up soon. Cops are here." As I moved out of the way of the squad car that was pulling up in the alley, they were hit with the high beams. All movement immediately stopped. They froze like deer stuck in the headlights. The added bonus was when the patrolman positioned his spot light directly on the shit show illuminating the ball of nakedness. As I walked by his window, I told him he might want some gloves for this event as it looks like a sticky situation at best. This was when one of the boys on the bottom asked if he could just finish up and then he would be happy to go away. I walked off into the darkness and laughed all the way back to the bar. I learned one thing that night; never think you have seen it all because the island will raise the bar.

Attack of the Wolf Pussy

The next insert also falls under the category of strip club firsts for me.

So this girl walks in; I seem to remember her from a few nights ago when she came in and asked for a job. At the time I told her to come back the next day at 7 P.M. Maybe she didn't understand the term next day; because it took her two days to come back or maybe she's on Island time. No one really knows. I'm thinking, hey she got the time right. One out of two isn't bad. So I tell her to go to the back stage. We talked for a minute and she informed me that she is a dancer from up north. I checked her ID and confirmed that she was of age, description matched the license she gave me, explained the rules of the club, handed out the commandments, and continued with the interview (yes gentle readers, strippers have an interview process too).

The next step in the hiring process is (of course) an on stage interview. The clubs in Key West are totally nude and we also sell liquor. Two things that usually don't go together, but then again, we're talking about Key West. We do everything a little different down here. In this club the first song is always topless, second song bottomless, just like the stage sets.

Now you may ask, "What the fuck, Chuck—a buck naked interview?"

To that I say, "Yes." And I'll explain. Not only do I run a totally nude strip club, I live in Key West and I have to make sure that the girls I hire are indeed uhh—how should I put this—girls. Gentle readers this is not a joke, and I have informed more than one dancer of the purpose for the try out stage set. Not only does it separate the rock stars from the groupies, but the main reason is that I have seen drag queens in Key West who have the ability to confuse the average sober straight guy. That being said, if I let a drag queen on my stage during operating hours not only would it be embarrassing as hell for me, and the club. It's a pretty safe bet that someone would end up in a fight, get hurt, and I would be out of a job.

On a good note it is Key West so if you're into that sort of thing I'll just point you in the right direction to the 800 block of Duval Street. Hey, we've got a little something for everyone in Key West. So anyway, I do my part and the machine keeps on running.

Now back to our girl on stage. Here she is, tromping around the stage not doing anything really impressive or spectacular. Normal shit that girls who have never danced before do. For example, attempt to copy moves that they have seen on MTV, BET or some other rock video—mostly horrible attempts at ass shaking followed up with a couple of deep knee bends and a lot of squat thrusts. In the grand scheme of things one could say it's nothing really sexy or alluring at all. But in these trying economic times she is a warm body, a hole and a heartbeat. And at the very least it would seem that she is attempting to get naked to a song, so far so good. Her first song ends and she looks at me with a blank stare, asking if she needed to continue. I reiterated the conversation that we had just had prior about my expectations, and the fact that this is a nude club not topless. I turn ask Rebecca my little fireball bartender to get me a Coke-a-cola. She fills my glass and hands me my drink. As I walk back towards the stage my gaze turns back towards the auditioning girl who is attempting to remove her pretty pink full bottomed granny panties and what do I see?

Wolf pussy!

What the fuck is happening here? Did I transport through time back to the 70's? This girl looks like she has Don King in a leg lock. She's rocking the full on sasquachian beaver.

So many things are running through my head as I resist the urge to just start laughing in her general direction while I hear Rebecca making telephone sounds in the background, "Ring, Ringgggggg, hey uh, the 70's called, they want their beaver back."

I'm also fighting the urge to shoot coke out of my nose; mostly because I have been in the strip club business for several years and the last time this happened was at least ten years ago when I actually took the girl back to the cat house and showed her how to operate a razor. Half a can of shaving cream and a couple of disposable Gillette's later she was ready to rock. That my friends, was an interesting event; seriously, I can't believe that I'm seeing it again.

I'm thinking, holy shit, what the Hell is that? Who does that anymore? What kind of bongo beating bimbo did the hippie bus drop at my door step? She has got to be fucking with me. Why doesn't she know about, or comprehend, female grooming standards especially if she had any inclination of getting a job at a strip club?

So I ask her, "Honey, when was the last time you shaved your box?" Hey cave girl, you're working a full set of pubic dread locks. I haven't seen a bush like that in about ten years and it wasn't good then either. It's just angry looking. Who fantasizes about a really hairy box? What kind of nasty bastard goes down on a pussy that looks like that? You have obviously spent a day or seven walking around the streets, living in a hippie bus, which is obviously not equipped with anything that resembles plumbing. There is nothing clean or sanitary about this situation. And, there is no way that thing is getting close to paying customers.

All righty then. Honey, interview is over. It's obvious that hygiene is not your friend. You need to shag ass back to the hippie bus, and I would suggest you grab a razor or three, some soap; both items are on sale at the local K-Mart. There's a public shower at the beach. If you want to work here, go forth and take care of business. Professional strippers don't do this shit. They clean up a bit, if you know what I mean. Go somewhere, fix your problem, slap on some war paint, wear the proper attire, so on, and so forth and come back when all that is done.

She then asked if I was joking. I told her no, not even a little bit. She said that she usually shaves prior to an interview, but for some reason did not this time. I had to look at Rebecca to confirm what I just thought I heard.

By the look of shock on her face I knew I wasn't hearing things and responded, "Seriously?" I'm thinking, yeah right; the last time you shaved that wookie cookie was years ago.

I then informed her of the numerous options of landscaping the nether regions if she was indeed actually thinking of attempting to work for me. Anything was better than this. Choices are many. The simplest and most effective would be downright bush eradication. You don't like the bald beaver thing? Get creative, trim it down then carve out a nice landing strip, a Hitler mustache, a little soul patch, a heart or an arrow pointing to your vagina. All are acceptable styles, but the full on 1970's free range beaver is not an option.

In my experience, Wolf Pussy has the potential to chase people away from the stage and that is counterproductive of the main goals of the establishment. Thanks for the interview and when you learn how to shave your box come back and we'll try this again if you want. I completed three more interviews after her, but she was the travesty of my evening.

Drink & Drown

The week in review; around 5,000 bikers came roaring into town for Bike Week. The S.D.V. (Seal Delivery Vehicles) guys are back in the keys for a little training, and a lot of drinking. All that, and the only problem I had was with a toothless bastard who is harassing us about the loss of his dentures during a drink and drown special. I met a man with a testicle the size of a tangerine, and I had to taze my buddy Corn Fed in the neck, and that's just the start of the week. You'll hear it again, "Key West, where the weird turn pro."

Let's start out with the dude with no teeth during drink and drown. Drink and drown is a special that the bar puts on to attract the cheap customers who want to get the most bang for the buck. You know the type, people vacationing on an extreme budget. It's usually the really young and the really old clientele. The reason is self explanatory. Young kids 21-25 are usually broker then a pick pocket in a nudist colony and budget their money accordingly (44 cents for ramen noodles, leaves me $12 bucks for beer money). The same goes for the older 55-65 years of age crowd. But these people usually have another issue that goes along with living here in the Keys (being homeless or residentially challenged, destitute, and oh yeah, drug or alcoholism to deal with). So as you can see, we get a good cross section of society, who's only interest in life is to get totally shit-housed drunk, throw up, pass out, fall down, and (of course) start the whole ugly process over again the next day on a very limited budget.

The bar being a licensed pharmaceutical representative for the distribution of alcoholic beverages is more than happy to help in that department. The more people we sell liquor to the more money in the boss's pocket and tips in the bartender's jar-o, and dollars in the dancers G strings. All of which, when combined pays the bills, keeps the lights on, and maintains the establishment for more amateur drinkers to congregate and partake in copious amounts of cocktails until the time that they either get their pro-card, or stop all together . It's a very vicious cycle, but as you can tell we're here to help.

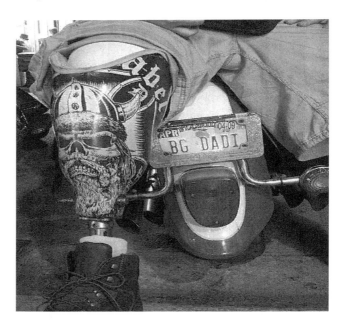

Dude, I've lost My Teeth

Now back to my derelict with no teeth. Antonio (one of my security guys and assistant manager at the time) would be the first to deal with this guy because it was my day off. You can't be the head honcho in the boner ballroom without a little down time. You will Fucking Die; if not from smoke inhalation, you'll just go crazy. Running a strip club or the bar business in general is full contact babysitting, while winding up the kiddies on high volumes of booze, Red Bull and whatever else they decide to inject, ingest, inhale, on their own. Is a recipe for disaster if any was ever there was one.

So, Antonio is tasked with solving this guys issues and the ass hat is speaking Swahili. Mumbling some intelligible bull shit that Antonio described as, "HMMMM, FFFNNN LLLSSST GGGURRGLE, TEEESPHHH." This witty banter went on for a few minutes before this pissy patron just got a pencil and paper to attempt to communicate the issue about losing his dentures and wondering where they were.

Just to let you know, my boy Antonio was one of those people who was lacking in the area of communication skills. His ability to communicate effectively with anyone, much less an irritating drunk with a horrendous case of halitosis, matched that of a claw hammer. He always had a very short temper, and today was not any different.

His not so subtle response was, "How the hell should I know, where the fuck you put your teeth, aren't they supposed to be in your mouth? How do you lose your teeth?" This, in my mind, is a very good question, but (of course) leads to the state of mind and the amount of booze this old bastard put down his neck hole the previous day. Of course, were not done yet. This will flow directly into the next level of paranoia. The old coot accuses Antonio of stealing his teeth. Yes it happens.

I call this the Democrat stage of being drunk. This is when the drunk decides to not take ownership of his/her actions and wants to place the blame on everyone but himself, and starts making outlandish claims like, "It's your fault that I got drunk." Or, "You sold me liquor to make me drunk." And, "I lost my dentures 'cause I was drunk on your property, so now you owe me a new set of teeth." Wouldn't you know it that is exactly what he said too? Needless to say he was ejected from the premises immediately and we never were able to find his teeth.

Friends Behaving Badly then Being Tased in the Neck.

Let me tell you about my good buddy Corn Fed. Everyone has a friend like this. Someone who usually would not hurt a fly, but like a gremlin has the unique ability to turn into an instant asshole just by adding copious amounts of liquor and feeding after midnight. Now, if you support this habit, your ass will have a gremlin tearing through the bar, but that is why we have security now isn't it?

In my buddy Corn Fed's case (as the name implies), is a large man. I would say about a biscuit shy of 400 lbs. Who is usually a teddy bear who sits in a corner and complains about world policies, government, the price of tea in china, or if the curtains match the drapes. He will come to your house, crash on the couch, raid the refrigerator, drink your orange juice, and complain that it has too much pulp in it, and then be pissy in general for a few hours until the next shiny object comes along.

All of this is normally in good fun, but under that cute cuddly exterior there is a grizzly bear sized gremlin just waiting to bust out and wreak havoc upon the world, especially when introduced to large quantities of fermented spirits and other beverages made with hops and barley, while shoveling down pieces of greasy pizza from Angelina's. This night was just a little different than most other times he has lurked in the shadows of the neon rainbow, swilling Crown Royal by the bottle at the bar. My man had just returned from a contract working in Asscrackastan somewhere. He was taking his drinking to an Olympic level.

Did I mention it was bike week? The bar was in full fucking swing. 500 bikers, 40 dancers, $1000 bucks on the desk in front of me, and my buddy good ole Corn Pone is apparently feeling neglected and wants to play grab ass with me. This type of action is mostly due to what I would assume, was the copious amounts of alcohol induction down his neck hole and all that contracting money burning a hole in his pockets.

Now just for shits and giggles I have to let you all know that I gave him the benefit of the doubt several times, but to no avail. His ability to comprehend that I was in the middle of something important, (like dealing with other people's money) was non-existent. His decision making skills were clouded. Add to that, the several scantily clad stripper types swarming in the area, and he apparently thought that he would impress them with his drunken bar antics by playing grab ass with the GM of the bar, who up to this point, has given his ass a lot of latitude with his indiscretions. He grabbed my ass several times, and he didn't compliment me on my game (I think it's like man rule #47 or something which specifically states if a man touches another man's ass and says, "good game" it's not gay).

I ignored him, which apparently only made him more aggressive. Then he decided that he was going to pull my pony tail. It was at this point that I reached down and tapped him in the nut sack. Not a full on nut shot mind you, just something across the bow, a grazing maneuver, to let him know I was getting over the bull shit. This action settled him down a little but then he ordered another shot of crown or something. It would seem the introduction of more alcohol allowed his freshly grazed balls to drop again.

I turned and gave my friend a good scolding. I advised that he should settle down, and stop fucking with me, "Can't you see that I'm a busy?" Well that's when the liquid courage to kicked in.

He grabbed me by the beard and asked, "What are you going to do about it?" God I love fucking drunks. If this was anyone else their ass would have already been handed to them. But this is my buddy. That being said, you still can't just do that shit to people. So I gave him a brief description of the future chain of events that were about to unfold in his world, and due to his lack of response, and now even tighter grip on my face armor, I knew that this would be one of those times that the old adage action speaks louder than words would come into play. I would simply have to show him. So, that is exactly what I did. I removed the little 650 KV Taser from my pants pocket and placed it in the left side of his fat bacon ass, grizzly bear sized, gremlin neck. I then gave him one last chance to let go of my beard. This was one of those opportunities that he just waved at as it blew right by him. He continued to smirk and again jerked my beard in a nice downward motion. I winked at him as I firmly depressed the trigger and let him ride the lightning.

Shockingly enough, (pun intended) the stun gun worked as advertised. I gave my buddy about two seconds worth of retribution, and a whole case of act right. Presto, motherfucking change-O I received instant gratification, and he got a pretty good education too.

Ladies and gentlemen, first you hear the noise, which is a very high pitched ZZRRRRRRPPTTT. Then I got to watch as his eyes rolled back in his head.

He immediately snapped to his senses, and complied with my previous verbal orders to let go of my beard, the whole time convulsing, coughing, gagging, spitting and snorting. He was in total disbelief that I was actually tasing him. All I can say is mission accomplished!
Poor old Corn Pone. When I pulled the taser away from his neck and broke contact with his skin he was mad as hell.

By that I mean my man was wrapped tighter then a coconut shoved up a monkey's ass. He could not believe that I shocked him.

His response was, "What the FUCK MAN? THAT'S FUCKED UP MAN! I can't believe you did that to me! God Dammit! FUCK! FUCK! FUCK!" He took a second or two, regained what was left of his bruised ego, and attempted to regain his composure, then immediately started mouthing off again, about how his ass took the ride and was still standing. Blah, Blah, Blah!

I informed him that he only received a couple of seconds worth of justice and that myself and Antonio (who had positioned himself directly behind Corn Fed) would be more them happy to engage once again and give him a more suitable dose of reality, and the rest of the club the show that they really wanted to see. Hell that would be the price of admission. Naked women, whiskey, cold beer and a sumo sized bar fight to close out the evening. That's something you don't see every day. Winning!!!

He turned and looked at my partner and came to the realization that the gig was up. We're no longer fucking around. You want to talk about immediate sobriety? What a buzz kill, and a total waste of beer money.

Now under normal circumstances good Ole Corn Fed would give you the shirt off his back; if he had a shirt that is. He has survived on the island for years longer than most people ever thought were possible. He is definitely another Key West survivor and a legend. I could write another book on his antics alone.

This man has worked every club on Duval Street three or four times. Once he managed to work two bars at the same time and was a full time mate on a fishing boat. I'm still not sure how that happened (only something Corn Fed could pull off). But I have to tell you his comedic value is unending. He is still one of my best friends. You know it's good when we can still laugh at drunken debauchery events, such as this one, and still maintain our friendship.

Stay thirsty my friend.

(I Never said you couldn't have fun at work.)

Tangerine Size Testicle

I met a man with a really large testicle. Now I know what you're thinking, what the fuck Chuck? How would you know that? I'm glad you asked, because I looked at it, that's how.

I had a guy come in (and Roper was his name-O), this particular gentlemen proceeded to lay a wager in my general direction, that he had the biggest nut (singular) that I had ever seen. I have to tell you all for some reason I have seen a lot of balls in the bar business—occupational hazard I guess. This was not the first, second, or third time someone wanted to solicit a free drink from the bar on an outlandish bar bet. Since I myself am a man with what I have been told are a really large pair of swinging, clanking balls, I could not pass up this opportunity to attempt to prove him wrong. So I called upon a slew of strippers who didn't have anything to do at that particular moment to witness the freak show.

Onward with the dick measuring contest and let's have a ball dangling good time while we do this thing. The parameters of the bet were set and captain testicle proudly produced one tangerine sized nut wrapped in one wrinkly scrotum sack.

There were a lot of OOOOS & AHHHHHS, a couple of OH MY'S and then one of my girl's (Sasha) said in a fine Russian accent, "That's not real." I had to agree with her. His enlarged fuzzy dangler looked more like something from a movie prop house than a real testicle. I had a drink on the line, so I'm not going to get worked out of a shot by some dip-shit and a prosthetic nut. I upped the game a bit. I proceeded to produced the rubber surgical gloves, applied them the way I had been taught in the academy, snapped the rubber cuffs with a little dramatic flair, and reached down and grabbed me a hand full of citrus sized nut and gave it a gentle tug just to see if it was attached, and to see what kind of response I would get from our boy. Surprisingly, when I tugged on his scrotum sack, he almost came off the bar stool. My question was answered and my curiosity was quelled. I ordered up the shot from Mrs. Suzy Q and pushed it in his general direction.

I took the gloves off shot them towards the nearest shit can, scratched my head and asked the obvious question, "You ever had that thing checked out? My best guess, and I'm no doctor or anything, but it looks like you got yourself a hernia, an infection, a little bit of both or something worse. I don't know what the problem is, but I know that something is not right." Amusingly enough, he was under the impression that even though his ball was 4 times the size of the other one, everything was alright. But wait there's more to my mutant freak show. Mr. Roper then proceeded to show me that he only has three toes on one foot too.

Response: "Hey Mutant, drinks on me." It's a small price to pay for entertainment like this.

My Friend Monster

So here is another one of those times that you have to just sit back and laugh. I was apparently having one of those nights. First we have ball sack boy, and now I have a group of guys who came in, bellied up to the bar, started talking loudly, and identifying one of their friends as Monster. This line of verbal bull shit went on for a couple of hours. Then one of the boys in the group decided to ask me if I knew why they called him monster. I looked in the general direction of the hundred and five pounds of flesh in a sock staring back at me. The general threat assessment was that I noted nothing out of the ordinary, and in my mind not a lot to be concerned about. Just your average pimply faced skinny fucker with greasy hair sitting at the bar looking drunker then a skunk.

So I said, "No, and furthermore I don't believe that I really care."

Then one of the guys said, "Hey how much do you want to bet that this guy has the biggest dick you have ever seen?"

Now I'm not sure what kind of bongo beating, hand holding, kum bi ya man love these guys were having with each other, but it was known that at the very least these guys at some point in time sat around and stared at each other junk, measured dicks, made estimations of relevant cock size and all agreed that Monsters' cock was bigger than all of theirs put together. It would seem they were all about celebrating too.

I replied to my new found friend and self nominated spokes person for the alleged John Holms Jr., "How would you know how many dicks I've looked at? Furthermore, why the hell would you think that I may want to gaze upon your newfound boyfriends meat missile in a club that is obviously for, how do I say this, straight guys.
Gentlemen if you have not noticed, I'm surrounded by naked women, I run a female strip club. You fellers may be

at the wrong end of the street." Now being an ambassador of goodwill and all that shit, I pointed out and provided the general directions to the Half Moon Saloon near the 800 block of Duval Street. I promised them that they could find all the assless chaps, leather caps, ball gags, and butt pirates a growing boy could want. "I'm sure if he is everything you say he is you can probably draw a crowd and make a little extra spending money, at the very least pimp his ass out for a couple of drinks. You know the same shit you're trying to do here. But be careful, you may just run into a little stiff competition."

One of my girls walked up and asks what they were talking about. Of course I took the opportunity to put Monster on the spot. I said, "I've been advised that good ole Monster here has the biggest cock that anyone has seen."

The spokesman then decided to pipe up and tell my associate that if she bought everyone a shot, Monster would show her his dick.

To which I had to reply, "Hold on cowboy. Which one of you fuckers has the big cock, you, your friends, or Monster here? If she is going to buy shots for everyone, you all have to drop your pants and well make it official. Biggest dick gets the drink. Give me a minute and I'll put you in front of the professionals here. Let me gather up the ladies let them get a couple of bucks together and put you boys on stage."

That's when the shit got real. All of a sudden the little dicks in the crowd shut up. By this time a couple of more girls arrived in my general area and asked what was happening, so I did the right thing and told them.

"Apparently Monster here has the biggest dick anyone has ever seen, or at least that is what his friends here claim." The problem is, Monster isn't saying anything, only his boyfriends are. So I started talking to monster directly and asked him, "Ok buddy we got you an audience. You going to sit there and stare at us, or are you going to pull out that magnificent meat stick of yours all up close and personal like, right out here in the neon light so the ladies can take a look at it? The rules are simple if in fact it is the biggest dick that they have ever seen you my friend will receive that shot from the bar, and they will buy you a shot or at least deposit a buck or two in those tighty-whiteys that you're so proudly sporting." Monster took a minute reflected on life, navel lint or something else, then asked if I was going to throw him out or beat him up.

I responded, "Hell no son you're officially part of the show. As I told you before I don't necessarily want to look at it but the ladies do, and if the ladies are happy that makes my job a whole lot easier. So unleash the weasel." Monster stood up, unbuttoned his Levi's, reached down his pants and started bringing out what looked like a baby elephants trunk holding an apple.

Boys and girls there were a lot of ooohs and ahhhs and I think I spouted out a good ole fashioned, HOLY SHIT! There I was looking at the dude's dick, while telling Suzy Q to bring me two shots. This ole boys meat stick was bigger than a baby's arm and smaller then a bread box.

One of my girls, Sasha (yes the same one as last time) said in her fine ass Russian accent, "Bullshit! That's not real." She reached out grabbed a hand full of limp lizard and gave it a tug, and wouldn't you know it; Monster just came along for the ride.

I started laughing and told Sasha, "If you do that a few more times he might owe you money." I looked at Monster and asked, "You don't get laid much do you?"

He said, "No not really."

I asked the girls, "Well, is it the biggest dick that you'll have ever seen?"

Most said yes, and one said no, but it is nice, and continued to ask, "Can you get it really hard?" We didn't get a reply from Monster as he stuffed his prick back into his pants leg. The girls tipped and paid up as expected. Shots were then lined up in front of him and his friends and the drinking began.

So I asked the obvious question to the ladies still standing around all wide eyed and amped up, "Would any of you fuck this guy?" A whole lot of hell no's came out of the crowd, I said, "Come on. I thought you ladies love the big cocks?" Nope. Nothing like that thing, it looks like it would hurt.
One of the girls said, "It's fun to look at but there is no fucking way I would let him split me open with that thing."

I asked Monster, "What the hell you do with that thing?"

He responded, "What the hell would you do with it?"

I replied, "Paint it green, put it on a leash and walk it down the street wearing a sign saying free pictures with my pet my iguana, and snap pictures of the event for posterity. Another option would be tie it in a knot and lasso onlookers. Maybe start a career in the real porn industry as the next big dicked bastard banging bimbos in rapid fire succession at Long Dong Silver productions."

Amusingly enough a couple of the girls took him back for a communal lap dance and to show him off to their other friends or something. When he got back to the bar, he continued to tell me that all nice girls wanted to do was to look at it.

"Sorry I'm laughing," I replied, " if I was a chick I wouldn't fuck you either."

He continued to loosen up as the drinks kept coming and told me that he's never had a real girl friend, just lots of one night stands. And most of the chicks that wanted him to have sex with them wanted it in the ass. I couldn't for the life of me figure that one out. But whatever.

He said, "A dick like this is a curse, I don't know what I'm going to do." He slammed another shot and pulled a couple of dusty dollars from his britches to tip the bartender. I suggested that I could put him on stage a couple of nights a week, call in the ladies and let them get an eye full. He could knock out a pay check and life as we know it would be good. Eventually he would find someone to take him on.

He respectfully declined my offer and said in true drunkenness, "Maybe one day I'll find misses right. But today I guess I have to settle for misses right now."

Poor Monster didn't last a whole lot longer. He eventually passed out at the bar and I had the boys carry him back home, or at least to the cab out the back door.

Life lesson 101: Ladies, don't judge a book by its cover. If you're ever sitting next to a skinny fellow, and just happen to give him a package check and there seems to be a little more bulge in the britches then what you're used to seeing, be careful you may have found a Monster.

I think I Want to Take it in the Ass

I had one of my girls (a long tall fiery red headed former school teacher) who was involved in a car accident in which she suffered a windshield taste test which caused some brain trauma, and the loss of her short term memory. Apparently another effect of the head injury was that she became obsessively horny all the time. Now when I say that, I mean nymphomaniac type insatiable weirdness. Girls, guys, threesomes, foursomes, and sometime more sums. So far don't sound so bad huh? Follow this malady with her short term memory loss.

Working with her was like an adventurous episode of ground hog day or 51'st dates. She would walk around topless tweaking her almost inch long nipples screaming, "I'm Horny, I'm Horny" to anyone within earshot. Then introduce herself to the bartender or any member of staff with whom she worked for the last 6 months or so. We learned to deal with it and work through the numerous reintroductions and drove on with life as we knew on a daily basis.

Well, one night she was telling me that her new boyfriend wanted to introduce her to the wonderful world of anal sex and butt plugs. He apparently wanted her to wear one while on one of their sexcapades, later that evening, and even brought her a bright shiny band new fresh out of the box butt plug to her while she was working in the bar.

So now she is walking around like a kid in a candy shop showing off her brand new black butt plug to everyone that will look at it and even some of the people who didn't want anything to do with it. Here's the problem: she informed me that she had never tried anal before, or couldn't remember it if she did (I guess there's an upside to short term memory loss) and was scared to try it, but did not want to disappoint her current BEAU. I informed her that she was asking the wrong person for advice about anything having to do with anal sex or the use of butt plugs. But in my opinion she had only two choices:

(1) drop her panties and stick it in her ass and walk around with it lodged up there as per the request of her new companion, or

(2) Don't.

It seems that I was not the only one that she had been complaining to about her butt plug problems all evening. After four or five hours of this everybody in the club was basically over it. So right around closing time one of my girls we will call "Madam H" and for the record, she is well versed in the fine arts of anything anal, she had apparently had enough and snapped.

She said, "For fucks sake. Give me that thing" then proceeded to snatch it away from the redheads' hands. She slapped the black rubber dong on the bar, pulled a condom out of her purse, professionally rolled the rubber over the butt plug, and applied liberal amounts of lubricant to the phallic device. She calmly walked up on the back stage, kneeled on a giant chair shaped as a high heal shoe covered in leopard print, looked back, spread her ass cheeks, and inserted it directly into her back door for everyone to see.

At that point she bent slightly forward at the waist, then spread her arms out to her side and said, "Ta Daaaaa!!! That's how easy it is." She then, pulled it out, stood up and removed the rubber and handed the butt plug back to its original owner and said, "See how easy that was? You think you can remember that?"

Crisis averted one class in full anal insertions complete.

Sphincter Flexing at the British Boys

As long as we're breaking in the backdoor end of the business, I have another story that just popped into my deviant little grey matter. This was some old school shit. One of the ladies that worked for me at the time Davian (pronounced DA-VI-an) was a cute little Marylyn Monroe wannabe. She was on the top tier of exotic, erotic, and totally psychotic dancers list. Her claim to fame was her famous winking sphincter act. This is where she would get on stage come up to a customer pull up her dress, expose her panty-less ass, widen her stance, bend slightly at the waist, reach back with both hands, and spread her butt cheeks so nothing was left to the imagination. Then she would begin to flex her sphincter muscle opening and closing her brown eye in rapid fire succession. There was a direct correlation to the amount of alcohol that was being consumed, the amount of money that was in front of you, and what you were willing to donate to the cause that gauged how close of a look you got, and how long that little show lasted. Some guys would keep her there for the whole set just staring into her ass. It was like they were trapped in a money sucking black hole and couldn't get out. She would just keep collecting the dollar bills as they fell on the floor and when the time was over or the tipping ended; she would slam the customer in the face with her ass cheeks damn near breaking their noses or necks, this movement definitely snapped them back into reality.

Now there was a similar show that was strictly saved for the gawkers. Same basic concept applies. She would lure one of these no money having dipshits away from whatever wall he was supporting first by targeting him and getting his attention. Making him believe he was the one that she wanted to show her goodies to (blowing kisses, winking, teasing and enticing) she would then continue by providing the bent over exposure of her bare naked buttocks, followed by that gentle come hither finger gesture movement which of course had the power to draw the target within range. She would give him the predominant quick peek at the puss and the show would begin. This is where it got interesting, if the target didn't make any attempt to locate his wallet or at the very least a couple of dollars didn't start to drop in what she considered a timely manner (usually 30 seconds) she would fart directly in his face. I'm not talking a little dainty girly poot, or some kind of pussy faced quaff. No sir. I'm telling you it was usually a Taco Tuesday, three bean burrito, butthole widening, certified trucker style ass ripping shit storm, which caused hairs to part, farticles to fly, and the smell could knock a buzzard off a shit wagon at 50 yards.

Amusingly enough if you watched closely, you could see it coming on the customers face. Their eyes would attempt to adjust to the darkness and they would attempt to focus on her pink puckering butthole actually getting sucked closer into the back blast area. Then the look of fear when that puckered asshole erupted, spraying noxious gasses and fecal fumes all over the subject's face was priceless. They would immediately fall backwards feverishly, wiping their faces, gasping for air, and crying out, "What the Fuck?"

At this point, Davian would calmly look up and say in her best little girl voice, "Ooops! Sorry." Or, "Its talking to you honey," while everyone else is pointing and laughing, gagging, coughing, or throwing money on the stage. And yes there were even a couple of guys who paid extra for this service.

So one day we get a British ship in town and the Brits—these guys, like most sailors who have been on a boat too long like to do three things—drink, fight and fuck. Needless to say we ended up with a fair amount of the crew in the club. Hell we have everything they want, beer, whiskey, pussy, and the illusion that they may get to walk out with some of it. If anyone needs a strip club its these guys. Just putting it out there the boys in the British Navy are not the pretties in the lot of prospective mates. Most come standard with bad teeth, bad breath, bad accents, and bad attitudes. I have to say I did not see any who would match the James Bond profile in this crowd.

Davian started her show and I just knew it was going to be an issue from the start. The target that she picked was a pissy drunken sailor who was slumped over at the bar slipping in and out of consciousness. She came over hiked her skirt, spread the cheeks and turned on the ass tractor beam. This got our boys attention. I watched as he began getting closer, and closer. Then all of a sudden I could see him focus. He stuck his finger in his mouth, pulled it out with a slippery wet popping sound, and jammed it second knuckle deep into Davian's turd locker. Then he looked at me and just smiled. Holy shit!! This fucker flipped the script. He successfully blocked the shit storm.

Davian obviously being surprised by the unexpected anal intrusion, shot across the stage like a rocket. Needless to say she was extremely pissed at the situation and fit to be tied. Hands, feet, fists and shoes started flying across the stage. And of course, I was the one expected to solve this little issue prior to it becoming a problem and possibly an international incident. Now I'll digress and tell you that Davian had been warned numerous times to not stick her ass this close to the customers. If she had been following the rules it would have been impossible for him to touch her. But now I have to enlighten my new found grinning friend on strip club etiquette. Especially the rule of, tip don't touch. There I am still laughing my ass off as I approached this gentleman and advised him of his indiscretions. Prior to me finishing my sentence he turned, looked at me and in a very harsh drunken British accent asked, "Who the fuck might you be?" Followed quickly with, "You look like a pretty big bloke, but I'll have a go at ya."

For some reason I knew this wasn't going to end well. The prick got up and took a swing at me. So before he could gather the brain cells and do it again, I snatched his ass up and started running for the first door I could find to crash into and I did exactly that. I began using my new found friend as a battering ram and to break my fall on the hard brick floor that I knew both of us were about to meet. As expected, I hit the door and it exploded open almost knocking it off its hinges. We hit the ground with a thud. Landing in front of the bar owner, and a couple of his friends (Joe and Sammy the sound man), I reached down grabbed his neck and punched him in the snot locker a couple of times to get his attention, turned him over and started to drag him out the door when Sammy said, in his best Americana surfer/stoner voice, "DUDE!!!!!! You just met the BIG STUD MAN!" I guess that answered his previous question. He was escorted out without any further issues.

Quotes from the Dali LLAMA:

So here we go, welcome to class ladies and gentleman:
Dealing with Drunks 101.

When dealing with large numbers of intoxicated ass-
hats or maybe one magnanimous asshole that was wearing
on your last nerve or pushing that one button you didn't
know you had, Dallas would be able to calmly say
something like this:

"We have done most of this shit to ourselves. We are
the licensed pharmaceutical representatives who allow these
people to get to their current intoxicated state of mind. It is
this state of mind that lowers the inhibitions, loosens the
wallets, and allows us to collect the income that we feel that
we so rightfully deserve."

So endith the lesson.

This was just one of my favorite quotes of inspiration
from the D.L L.L.M. (Dallas, the Luscious Loving Llama
Mama). This woman is a Key West Legend and stripper
extraordinaire. Please allow a little clarification here.
Dallas by definition was not a stripper. She was a woman
who striped for a living. She was not just another pretty
face. She was what we call a triple threat; drop dead
gorgeous, 5'8" of rocking bombshell who worked the double
D's like it owed her money, and had an ass you could
bounce a quarter off of (I did once or twice, maybe even
three times). She had more energy than a stick of dynamite.
When she took command of the stage, worked the runway,
took a spin or two on the pole the money would be liberated
from

loosened wallets in rapid fire succession from the fantasy stricken onlookers all over the club. Those poor bastards never saw it coming. When Dallas came for your money she worked you hard, and wasn't satisfied until she got your wife's Christmas money, your kid's lunch money, and your cab fare home out of your sock. The customers always felt good about giving until it hurt. Well at least until the next morning, but by then it was too late.

That, my friends, is a real life professional. She possesses a lot of common sense in this uncommon world, and has more life experience then you could load on a dump truck. She is legend in the business and a mentor to a lot of the dancers in the club who would search her out and seek her advice. Dallas would do everything she could to help guide you down that path, and open your eyes to the world around you. She was brutally honest, but sometimes people need that kind of honesty to evolve into a better person.

The Llama is a great listener (the best friend I have ever had), and is good with sayings that make you think, and help to guide you through stressful situations in life. Remember there are always several paths one can take—one just has to choose the correct path.

Fantasy Fest Week

So it's Fantasy Fest and as most of you know, this is the super bowl of weirdness. For the uninitiated or those of you who have never been, the best description is Mardi Gras without the crime. It's a 10 day long Halloween party full of costumes, or not. Most of the revelers just come down south, take their clothes off, and slap on liberal amounts of body paint. For some revelers the less costume, the better. So, if you come down here during October you better come to party. And for God sakes, leave your moral fiber and your kids at home; you won't be needing any of that here.

The worst are the guests who arrive and bring their children, complain that everyone is naked, people are assholes, and kids shouldn't see this kind of stuff going on. They are the ones who want someone to clean up the streets, and make statements like, "Doesn't anyone have any decency or self respect anymore?"

These are the people that I stare at like a hog looking at a wrist watch. Then these questions flow through my mind:

(1) Is this your first Fantasy Fest?
(2) If so, did you not read the brochure?
(3) Did you suffer some sort of tragic head injury resulting in amnesia caused by passing out the last time you came to Fantasy Fest?

Or my all time favorite:

(4) Are you a fucking retard?

If the answer to all the above questions was NO, then your ass is just a booger eating moron who gets exactly what you deserve. You should have done your homework prior to planning a vacation to Adult Disneyland. This is one of the only places in the continental United States where you can get away with the shit that we do here. People know that, and that is exactly why they come back year after year, and pay $300, $500, and $700 dollars a night in our not so luxurious hotels.

If you answered yes to any of the above questions, you need to be removed from the gene pool. Unfortunately because you have the children with you, that means that you have already bred and passed your flawed DNA down the chain of command. Hell, your retarded son will probably run for president and have the same problem understanding the laws of probability that you did.

Here's a note—Fantasy Fest has not changed a thing for the last 30 years with the exception of removing more items of clothing, adding body paint, and more choices of liquor to drink. The fact is more people come to see and participate in the event every year, bringing with them, hundreds of thousands of dollars in much needed revenue to help stimulate our little islands' fragile trickle down economy during the slow season.

What kind of a parent are you?

If one or both of you were here sometime in the past, lets say 10, 20, or even a year or so, have you forgotten that not so many years ago, you were the ass clowns who were doing the same exact thing as the heathens you're now complaining about. You guys were running down Duval Street with a beer in one hand, and a 15" double headed black dildo in the other, while still leading your husband/wife or significant other through the crowds of humanity wearing nothing more than a leather vest, assless chaps, and a ball gag. Now you're acting appalled? Get the fuck out of here! Did you find your moral compass in a closet, or lose your personality in a card game? It's very simple, if you want to be naked in public come on down. If you want to get drunk in public—come on down. If you want to see naked drunk people or be naked and drunk in public—come on down. If you are offended in any way shape of form by drunken naked people in public—DO NOT COME DOWN FOR FANTASY FEST.

This is not the vacation for you.

So now that you have the disclaimer down we can get to some of the weirdness that happened in the club. I'll start you off with the moderate exhibitionist & chronic masturbators who arrive on scene and hit the real perverts later.

Cock Sock

Exhibitionist: simply put the people who enjoy being watched. One example is: Cock Sock guy. He's a veteran of many Fantasy Fests and returns every year just to get his freak on. Now when I say cock sock that is exactly what this guy was wearing. More importantly, that is all he was wearing. You guessed it, a sock over his extremely large cock—and I don't mean chicken either.

How would I know that you ask?

Well I had the pleasure of being called to a disturbance involving this guy massaging his fuck muscle right in front of the DJ booth, of course miraculously when I got there, he would stop, and act as normal as a man wearing nothing but a cock sock sporting a hard on could act.

Now when you run a totally nude strip club as I did at the time, one of the main concerns is not really if a guy is sporting wood or not, its where does this guy keep his wallet and did he pay the cover charge? And two, keeping this type of shit contained so no one gets really offended or hurt. Hey, it's a Key West freak show; as long as it's contained we don't have a problem. It's when our boy takes out his cock, ties a lasso around the end of it and attempts to rope the innocent passersby, or when he decides to go to the private dance room with one of the girls. That, my friends, is when it becomes an issue.

Do you remember my first question? Where does he keep his wallet?

Third is what's going to happen if he actually gets excited? Look at the size of that fire hose. Who's he going to use it on when it graduates from its current status of baby's arm holding an apple to a fucking fully fledged Louisville Slugger? Anyway, standard protocol states I keep an eye on our boy.

Later on in the evening he found a dancer who tickled his fancy and he picked out a little girl named Scarlett, who was a tiny, skinny, little thing, all 80-95 lbs of her. Apparently her mind was on the money and figured what the hell. I watched as she took rocking cock-socking Jonny Holms here to the back room for a little $20 dollar boom, boom and started the session. As soon as Scarlett commenced to get her grind on and began shaking her little booty to whatever beat box base lines, techno taunts, or rock & roll rhythms, which may have been blaring over the speakers to set the mood for her next adventure in a $20 dollar three minute romance, pants off, dance off session. At that time, let's just say, nature took its course. Wouldn't you know it, shit started to happen. Needless to say the dance didn't last but about a minute. That's when our friend started reenacting scenes from Anaconda. His sock started moving. He apparently wanted to show poor little Scarlet a couple of moves that he learned when he was dancing for Thunder from Down Under about 20 years ago.

So Long Dong Silver jumped up and pushed Scarlet to the back of the booth. He then whipped off his cock sock and started swinging his root around like Darth Vader wielding a light saber, making stabbing motions towards poor Scarlet's face. I'm watching all this unfold on the video cameras. W.T.F! I knew this was gonna be bad when I saw little scarlet suck back to the wall in horror attempting to dodge the dick almighty, because you know its shit like this that can put a girl's eye out. Nobody wants that to happen. One eyed strippers, or performers who look like they just took an ass whooping from a pimp are bad for business.

I get to the back room where this guy is now beating his dick like it owes him money (amusingly enough at this point it was going to). I grab him by his neck and what was left of his 1980's mullet, restrict his airway just a little to get my point across, and start to drag him to the first available exit, as he is still in full jack mode. He was so enthralled in the Situation I don't think he noticed me dragging him out for the first few seconds or so. He may have even switched hands and gained a stroke or two on me while enroute to the exit door. I bowled over three or four people who just wouldn't move. When my partner arrived, I'm not sure what he was thinking, but I do know that he put a flash light in this guys side and told him that if he moved or got any dick on him (pun intended I'm sure) he was going to light him up. I'm sure ye ole wanking boy thought he had a Taser in his side so all violent repetitive motion stopped on his part. I'm still attempting to stretch his neck, in order to get him and his pet iguana to the door. Upon arrival we sent him and his sock urban surfing down Charles Street. That is a nice way of saying he was thrown out of the club wearing nothing but a limp dick and a smile. Needless to say, he is not going to be invited back until next Fantasy Fest.

Note: Boys and girls if you can make a stripper run away from a lap dance and hand full of hundreds you have done something wrong.

Love Notes

Prior to getting into the love notes, I have to explain the theory of the love note. It's like a stripper pass down log, a to/do or maybe a do not do list. This paperwork is a list of weird occurrences that one would only expect to happen in a strip club. One that normal people would never expect at all.

This is how it works. If I had something that I wanted to communicate with a girl or the girls, instead of having a daily meeting, I would simply type it up, print it out, and tape it to the dressing room mirrors, for all to see. This form of communication solved a lot of potential problems. It lets the ladies know I was paying attention, answered relevant questions, and provided the plan of the day.

Here are a few examples of what I would call the best of the love notes:

Love Note

Ladies: you may or may not have noticed; we had a dancer that had a little weight issue, who is no longer with us. The indicator: <u>if you happen to be wearing a school girl skirt and are unable to zip it closed because your ass had doubled in volume since you wore it last</u>. That is an indicator that you are in desperate need of a wardrobe change, a new diet, and a workout plan, or all of the above.

Note to self: toilette paper and tampon strings glow in the black light. Baby wipes are your friend, dingle berries are not. They tend to affect your money! There are several mirrors strategically placed around this dressing room and are for your viewing pleasure. Use them. If you can't see your own ass, ask a friend to check it out for you, and then get a second opinion. If you get on stage and have forgotten any of these steps, the customers will instantly let you know about it. You will know there is an issue by the loud roars of laughter or customers running from the stage pointing in your general direction trying not to shoot beer from their noses. This falls under hygiene and maintenance. Do not let this happen to you.

Love Note

Bodily Secretions: more importantly, Urine: ladies it would seem that every time I think that I have seen it all, someone comes along with something that is able to shock the hell out of me. So I first want to congratulate one of you personally for this milestone of achievement. Congratulations, you have made the love note.

Case in point, If you have ever gone to work, and got so intoxicated that you walked around naked, blathering some nonsense about lifting your left breast in the midday sun and possessing Voodoo Pussy, then lost control of your bodily functions and urinated on the floor, and then pissed into the trash can some of your coworkers strategically placed directly beside the unoccupied toilet and had the audacity to blamed it on a white devil slave master or the demon that lives inside you. I'm here to tell you, just in case you don't realize it:

THIS IS AN ISSUE!

If you have done it TWICE in the same week, I'm here to tell you that it is an abomination!!! By definition: something that causes great disgust. Oh, note to self, alcohol is no longer your friend…If you would like a recap of the incident I do have the raw video footage of the event that you described as a "**demonic possession**" for your viewing pleasure.

This issue has been brought to my attention and I have been advised by your co-workers that they are not into the whole *Golden Shower Scene*.

After further consultation, I have also been advised by your co-workers that in order to receive pleasure from a golden shower one has to:
(a) Be into golden showers,
(b) Pick the person who is giving the golden shower, &
(c) Be paid extra.
By the very fact that I was the one mopping up the puddle of piss on the floor, you will be paying me an extra janitorial fee.

Since I believe that no lesson is learned until you have suffered emotional or monetary loss I'm going to double tap you with that fee to make sure that this lesson is compounded and learned as soon as possible.

This note will cover the emotional part, your fine which (of course) will be paid directly to me. Let me see how you put it, Oh yeah; Your White Devil Slave Master for my

Janitorial consultation fees will cover the monetary portion of your learning issue. Remember:

Stripping is a Full Contact Beauty Contest.

Love Note

Retirement

<u>I know it's an ugly thought for some of the ladies here.</u> The question is how do you know when or if it's time to hang up the spurs, high heels, fuzzy slipper, or the good ole T-back thong?

I'm sure that question has been contemplated by everyone here, but it's a question that needs to be answered, and like everything else I'm here to help. There are two types of retirement. First selective, and second would be known as mandatory retirement.

The first will be retirement on your own accord. This is when you recognize that you are no longer physically or mentally into this business any more. You can't handle the crowd, the people, the girls, the bar, the smoke, or the bull shit any longer and it's time for you to move on. If you have done right by yourself, stuck to your plan, saved your money, bought a house or rental properties, put money away in savings account, made some good investments, bought a business or married a millionaire, it would be safe to say that you can relax in luxury for the rest of your days. The answer is simple, retire whenever you want to.

Mandatory retirement: may have some of the same qualities as selective, but unfortunately due to circumstances that may or may not be in your control, or just piss poor planning and bad judgment calls, you are not able to stop dancing. Or you are unable to recognize the problem is YOU!

How to recognize that you are no longer cutting it in the world of strippers? Characteristics include but are not limited to:

You hate your job. You hate the customers. You hate the club, or you are negative towards everything listed above at the same time. These are some more indicators that you are about to be retired, put out to pasture, and forced to work elsewhere. Other indicators as listed may include:

(1) You have to inject, ingest, inhale, large amounts of legal or illegal drugs to make it through a night's work.

(2) You no longer have the ability to consistently pay $32 dollars House after being at work for 7 hours. Then want to place the blame on everyone else (managers, DJ's, staff, & customers). Ladies that is one lap dance and $12 dollars from a stage set. If you can't pull that kind of money, you're in the wrong business.

(3) Customers consistently tell you how pretty you are and then as soon as you leave immediately dance with anther dancer.

(4) Customers consistently leave the stage as soon as you approach it.

(5) Customers consistently, point, laugh, and run away, when you approach them. Or if they stay ask questions like:
   (a) Are you a man?
   (b) Are you pregnant?
   (c) Will you have sex with them in their trailer, vehicle, parking lot or back alley for $20 bucks?

(6) To prevent these questions, we have to knock out all the lights prior to getting on stage.

The solutions for some of your problems are listed:

Q: What if I can't make house?
A: Go to day shift, there is not house fee charged on day shift.

Q: What if I'm FAT?
A: Put the fork down, diet, exercise, and corsets will help you.

Q: What if I'm ugly.
A: Well I'm not sure how you made it this far. My suggestions—be nicer, use your sense of humor, and find a personality.

Q: What if I stink?
A: Go immediately back to the basics. Wash the smelly parts of your body with soap and water, dry the affected area; apply liberal amounts of powder, perfume or deodorant. Repeat as necessary. If that does not help solve your problem, call your physician and schedule an appointment. If none of that works, just practice the phrase "paper or plastic" to prepare for your next line of work because your days here are numbered.

Love Note

Ladies, as you now know Princess is gone.....

Why you may ask? Because she was being a bad dancer, over charging the customers, and promising them shit she could not legally do. We do not promise to make guys cum! We do not charge over $20 dollars for one private dance.

Why you may ask?

Because it's bad for business; if you piss off a customer because you are a greedy fucking cunt they will not buy another dance from you or any of the other dancers in here. They will then tell their friends about your ass and they will not buy dances from you or the other dancers or drinks from the bar, and more importantly they will not come back. As you can tell this type of behavior is bad for everyone. If the bar fails, you fail.

Warning: if I think that a dancer is ripping off a customer I will set her up to fail by using a spotter. If you fail you will go away.

Stripping Is a Full Contact Beauty Contest.

Love Note

Ladies; Happy Valentine's Day. First issue of the evening: sometimes I say things that I think really should remain unsaid. But then an event happens, that removes all doubt and it falls within the parameters of my job.

Calls of nature: dropping a deuce, taking the kids to the pool, copping a squat, taking a crap, pinching a loaf, grinding one out, or just good ole fashioned taking a shit. Usually on this planet such an intimate act requires a little privacy, and in such cramped quarters as this dressing room, I would assume is most appreciated by your coworkers. The only times that I can think of that it would be acceptable to take a shit with the curtains or the door open is if you are in prison or the comfort of your own home, or you have some pervert paying you a lot of extra money to perform that service for him/her.

And now for the list of Don'ts. Let's review:

- Don't let a customer touch your pussy.
- Don't touch a customer's dick or pussy.
- Don't kiss a customer on the lips with or without tongue. (Do I really have to write this shit?)
- Don't scream, push, and shove customers or other employees any time.
- Don't promise customers anything that you are not willing to back up just to get them to the champagne room. If you promised a blowjob, anal, oral, a threesome, foursome or that you will dress up in a fucking clown suit, take care of your business somewhere other than this club. If I get a charge back I'm taking it out of your wallet.
- Don't forget to get your money up front. That means prior to the dance.

- Don't forget to get naked. This is a nude club, second song is always bottomless. Both stages.
- Don't interrupt a champagne room while a dance is in progress.
- Don't forget to pay your bar tab.

Love Note

Ladies; backroom squabbles are a no-go. I would like to see the return of the good ole fashioned guerilla warfare type private dance. This has a simple meaning:

- Do your assessment; is your customer a gawker, a goober or a $$$Smooooooooww$$$$? This would be the quick peek in the wallet to count the money, credit cards, or coins of the realm. How good of a customer can this guy be?
- Now close the deal and assault the wallet by getting your money up front.
- Seal the deal. Do the dance, take care of business and get the hell out. Otherwise known as the GHQ (Get it, Hit it, and Quit it).

Oh and keep your head out of the customers crotch. What are you looking for down there? Why are some of you putting face in some total strangers sweaty, stanky, danky, musty, dusty walking on Duval Street cock locker or sweat box?

Hygiene: ladies due to the amount of girls who are currently in the dressing room, I have been advised that I apparently have to offer some advice to a couple of ladies regarding personal hygiene, AGAIN.

1. In America, bathing daily is a requirement. Soap and water usage is a plus.

2. Wash all costumes and shoes as necessary. Dr. Scholl's and Lysol do wonders for hoof rot, or stink foot.

3. If you can't take a bath because you're residentially challenged or you're living in your car, cologne or perfume is your friend. I would rather you smell like a French whore in a brothel then a Key West street performer after a midsummer show at Mallory Square.

Sex Fact of the Day:

Some professionals consider masturbation to function as a cardiovascular workout. Not including foreplay the average sex session lasts about seven minutes.

7 Minutes….Boys, here's the lesson. Remember all that shit you heard in high school gym class or the locker room about banging some chick for hours and she loved it. Well it was BULLSHIT!

Love Note

Pissing in the sink is unacceptable!

I have to say congratulations this is another first in the business. You know who you are, and everyone else does too.

Secondly, were you raised by fucking troop of baboons?

Third, I want you to know that I do not give a fuck about excuses at this point. I don't care if your mom didn't hug you enough or that your dad didn't like you, or you have a fucked up phobia of public toilets.

I just want to know what third world shithole you came from? This is unacceptable and you owe me fine money and lots of it or hit the fucking bricks and piss in someone else's sink you nasty fucking crack head.

For your education I guess that we have to define sink, so here it is:

Sink: by definition is: a bowl shaped fixture that is used for the washing of hands, face or small objects. Notice it specifically stated that it is used for washing hands, face, small objects. Not pissing into because you're too nasty or lazy to squat or hover over the toilette.

Toilette: a fixture used for defecation and urination, consisting of a bowl fitted with a hinged seat and connected to a waste pipe and a flushing apparatus.

Stripping is a Full Contact Beauty Contest.

Love Note

Stage Clearing Sea Donkeys

Its spring break time again. Some of you ladies have, let's just say, packed on the poundage over the winter. So the scale will be coming back out of the closet. If the current number is greater than the old number, you will be taking a break to complete a mandatory PT program of bicycling, weight training, and yoga, whatever it takes for you to drop back within the weight standards.

Some indicators that you may recognize that will in fact clarify that you have become a **Stage clearing Sea Donkey:**

1. If you get on stage and the customers leave.
2. If the customer has to ask if you're a man.
3. If the customer tells you your butt is bigger than his buddies who is the truck driver sitting next to him.
4. If you start rocking a (Fat Upper pussy Area) F.U.P.A. or beer gut over your school girl outfit.

Note: when you clear the stage it takes about nine minutes for the customers to come back. That's about three songs or $60 bucks.

I will not penalize the ladies who work out and take care of themselves for a mule team of sea donkeys. You chose this profession act accordingly.

Stripping is a Full Contact Beauty Contest.

Love Note

Ladies your ass cracks do not have a magnetic strip attached to either side. If they did, it would be acceptable for the customer to swipe his credit or debit card. Since that is not the fact, it's not allowed. Furthermore, do not allow the customers to swipe dollar bills between your ass cheeks either. Only bad things can come from this. Least being a nasty paper cut on your pretty pink parts.

Next: I was contacted by Shay, who asked me to please pass on a message. Whoever is texting or calling her please stop. Apparently Shay does not have the ability to lock her phone or keep it away from her child. Her child is getting all the texts and calls. Including but not limited to:

1. Pictures of chicks with large gaping assholes (it is unknown if this is a medical problem or very extreme sex act).
2. Pictures of horses with dicks that touch the ground, again unknown on the type or breed of horse we're talking about.
3. Bestiality or porn shots.
4. Bukake video.
5. Butt plug shots.
6. And finally something with a disturbed clown in it.

Shay did mention that she would be more than happy viewing these items on your phone but do not send it to hers.

Stripping is a Full Contact Beauty Contest.

Tasers, Stun Guns, Buttholes, Beavers, and Bar Games

Let's talk about bar games. This particular one is called Surrender.

We will start explaining the rules. First there are two types of Surrenders in this particular bar game.

Type 1 is called the Full Personal Surrender.

Type 2 is a bar, place, or object Surrender.

I can hear you all screaming; what the hell is a Surrender?

Well just stay seated, I'm about to tell you.

This is a game that was, to my knowledge, originated and was invented by a couple of guys here in the fabulous Keys, Adam and Dave. I would guess an offshoot of planking but better, and then it sort of caught on. With the help of the internet, it has been around the world. It would be safe to say that these boys have way too much time on their hands, and we could write a whole book about Surrendering itself.

This is how it goes, as described by Dave himself so pay attention.

Part one of a good personal Surrender is of course the uncomfortable stretch. I can hear your questions now, how can a stretch be uncomfortable? Well this is the explanation. You have to totally invade the personal space and privacy of someone who you do not know at all, then of course you are willing and able to take the ramifications of such action. Be that a slight push, all the way to punch to the head. That being said, a person practicing an uncomfortable stretch will get face to face up close and personal like with another drunk patron, customer, employee at the bar, and start bending side to side, like he/she is warming up for a local sporting event.

Note: this action will usually get a drunks attention after about the third uncomfortable nipple brushing event.

Next will be the eye lock. Just to make sure that your mark is paying attention to you and is focused.

Immediately after that will come either some sort of squat thrust maneuver, deep knee bends, or another calisthenics type move normally called cherry pickers (look them up). So if the one who is now doing the Surrender is not engaged in mortal combat at this point, let's just say the other party or the mark as I like to call them is either:

(A) not paying attention or
(B) is attempting to get the hell out of the way cause he thinks his ass has wandered into the wrong bar and is in need of and emergency egress plan.

If you think that we are done, I'm here to tell you that you are totally wrong and have not been paying attention. The icing on the cake is what we call the Full Surrender. Directly after the circus side show action of human flexibility the person who is doing the Surrender will then face plant in almost a total supine position, face down on the floor in whatever is located on the floor at the time, cigarettes, beer swill, puke, piss, dirt, dust, grime, and bar filth in general. The Surrenderers arms are flung backwards, palms up, knees on the ground, now coming up to more of a downward dog like yoga position. The back is bent, thrusting the ass up in the air. And that my friend is a Full Surrender. As you will notice demonstrated on the bar by none other than Dave, the master himself.

Of course the second version is far less offensive but equally as amusing. This type of Surrender can be done almost anywhere: bar tops, bathrooms, statues, saunas, road signs, parking lots, bakeries and steam rooms.

It would seem that the boys have dedicated this to be their lives work, or at least their life's work for the upcoming year. And it has taken off.

People are surrendering everywhere. If it's a monument, road sign, or something of importance, you can bet that someone will be doing, or has done Surrender on or around it.

I'm proud to say that I myself have even been the victim of one of Dave's Full Frontal Surrenders. Continue reading and you'll see how getting caught up in the moment and lack of situational awareness will get you in trouble.

Dealing with Democrats and Sudden Surrenders

The issue was that I was dealing with a customer at the time; and this poor excuse of a human was attempting to get me, as the manager of the Club, to buy him a free beer. You may be asking why I would want to do such a thing. The answer is, I wouldn't. I don't just buy random customers beers for the simple reason that it cuts into the overhead and my employer would have an issue with that. Anyway, this poor S.O.B. is attempting to explain that he left his beer lying on a table for about five minutes, and now it's gone; someone has taken it and he would like another one.

So I break into the sermon and begin to preach the gospel of the church of the failing liver, according to the rules of strip club etiquette on, how is this possibly my fault? I start going over the facts just to see if I'm missing something pertinent. You have already told me that:

(1) You left your beer all alone on a table and walked away? If you really cared about your beer, why would you just leave it lying around? Hell, with that kind of an attitude, I don't think that you really deserve another beer. You, my friend, are not a responsible beer drinker. You just leave your beer where-ever and hope it can survive on its own out here amongst all these obviously thirsty beer drinkers. I need you to look around; do you see all these people here drinking beers?

Customer: "Yes."

Me: "Have you questioned any of those people?"

Customer: "No!"

Me: "Do I have a Beer?"

Customer: "NO!"

Me: "Then how did I get into this? Why would you think that I'm going to give you a beer to replace the fictitious beer that you may or may not have left laying around? Is this something that you do often? And does this ever work? I'll bet you're a democrat?"

Customer: "What? Uhh, why would you ask that? How did you know I was a democrat?"

Me: "Well that would be the only way that any of this shit would make sense. You see for some reason, I only get stupid requests like this from democrats. For some reason you people think that it's always someone else's responsibility to take care of your shit, your issues and your problems. That being said, my friend, I'm not sure that I can help you, but what I can do because I don't want to lose your business is I'll allow you to buy another beer and see if you can hold on to the next one. You know, be responsible for something in your life, keep it until it's gone, don't let anyone else hold on to it for there are many like it, but this beer will be yours. Hell you can even name it if you want."

I look down and what do I see; Dave in mid-Surrender.

It was at that point, that I realized that I had become the mark (remember that surrender shit you were just reading about). Yes, boys and girls, it would seem that my buddy Dave was in mid-Surrender. As you can tell, my boy Dave does not have very good timing. He was just getting into improper stretch placement; yep full on nipple rubbing action. Add to this, the poor customer we have been talking about. This guy was attempting to grasp the horrible reality that he was not getting another beer.

Dave then dropped into squat thrust position, whipped a 180 degree turn, and dropped into full Surrender. Yep, right there on the bar floor full-O-beer filth, swill, and whatever else is there. Now my ass has totally forgotten about my little drunken democrat bar patron and my full attention is, of course, on Dave.

RETRIBUTION!

You, my friend, are not going to make an ass out of me in the Club that I run. How can I turn the tables? What do I have in my little arsenal? My mind is a blur with options. Gentle readers if you haven't picked it up by now, I'll have to tell you, I still own a sense of humor. I too, like a little fun and if someone is going to make me a mark I'm going to attempt to turn the tables a bit.

I already have the ability to have just as much fun with Dave, as he is having with me. And the opportunity has presented itself in the form of a drunken man laying on the floor, ass up, and I have my hand firmly planted on my 650,000 volts of stun gun and it is coming out of my pocket with such ease. It's like I have practiced this move several hundred times before. The Stun gun is ready for a little light show and electro shock therapy. Now all I have to do is reach down and shock Dave directly in the ass, and that is what I immediately did. The stun gun fired off, ZZZZZZRRRRRRRRRPPPP, and it worked as advertised. I provided my boy with a couple of seconds of Key West shock therapy to get his mind right. Cops and criminals call this demonstration "riding the lightning." As Dave started levitating approx three feet off the ground he screamed, "OUCH!" then asked, "What the fuck was that??"

When I stopped laughing, I said, "About 650,000 volts." The poor customer that I had recently been dealing with looked at me like I had lost my mind. I then asked him if he still needed help in getting another beverage.

He shook his head in the compass directions of east and west and verbally stated, "Nope. I'll get it myself."

That, my friends, was what I call a lesson in— DIPLOMACY—the fine art of letting someone else gets your way.

Full Vaginal Tasing

Continuing on with the previously scheduled program; it just so happened that one of the girls, Madam H, who was overseeing the commotion of Dave on the ground, came over and said, "You had me at ouch." She started asking Dave questions like, "How did it feel? What happened? Did he want to do it again?" She then looked at me and asked "Do you think that would hurt if I let you shock my pussy?"

I attempted to laugh it off thinking that she was joking, and said, "Hell yes it will hurt! I mean look at Dave here. I'm sure his ass still has a little twitch and tingling sensation to it; and you want a full on shot to the crotch? Hey, I'm here to help. I'm a fine provider of fantasies, dreams, and a few kinky fetishes, too. When you think you're serious I'll be here to push the buttons."

Boys and girls, you can't make this shit up. Truth is stranger than fiction. Madam H came back the next night about 03:30 a.m. and pulled my card. The Bar was dead. We had 2 customers and the crew. She came up told me that she was ready to test the stun gun. I said sure, and whipped it out. Half way expecting her to chicken out, but somehow knowing that she wouldn't at the same time. She got on the stairway entrance to the stage, spread her legs and exposed the beaver. Now this is not the normal beaver. When I say that, it comes with all kind of accessories in the form of aftermarket products (I mean piercings to be more precise). Or as Madam H likes to call them "eating utensils) I think the count was four labia, and one hood, but you know I may have lost count. Let's just say there was a lot of metal in the business area. Hey, everyone needs to accessorize something every now and then. Who the hell am I to pass judgment?

As you may have figured it didn't take long to gather a crowd. It's like a train wreck—some people don't want to look but you just have to. Madam H then asked me if I could arc the piercings. I told her that on the first time it may not be a good idea (like getting a stun gun to the snatch is ever a good idea). But as you may be guessing Madam H may have a little freak in her. From the looks of things, I apparently, have the unique ability to help bring that freak out. Who the hell am I to tell her that we probably shouldn't do this? I mean the bar is officially closed, we're both consenting adults, she don't mind the crowd, and I know it's not going to kill her.

I tell her that I'm not going to hit the hardware. We're going to have to do a test run and I'm going to what is called a dry stun so she can have a taste of the action. A dry stun is when the contacts of the stun gun make skin contact. You know the same thing that made Dave levitate and scream like a girl in the previous story?

Side Note: It's not necessarily the pain involved with getting stunned. It's the noise that freaks most people out. The second thing is the sight of lighting, or the electricity arcing and sparking. You have to understand, that people in general since the beginning of time do not like three things: heights, loud noises, and fire.

I'm using two out of the three aforementioned items; lightning or the visual sight of electricity arcing between the points is, in this case, the fire. So I light up the device. It comes to life making that ZZZZRRRRPPPP! Sound that we have all become strangely familiar with. Nothing! She does not even flinch. I then place it gently between her legs in her pubic area, and firmly depressed the trigger. Again the Stun gun came to life. ZZZZRRRP. She jumped, but just a little. I let go of the trigger, and rocked back expecting to block a leg attached to 6" stiletto spiked healed platform shoes coming across my face area. I looked at her and she started laughing. Amazed at what I just did, I hear one of the doormen say, "That was a full vaginal tasing." The whole bar crew just burst out in laughter.

Madam H without skipping a beat looked at me and said, "Well that didn't hurt as bad as I thought, kind of like laser hair removal." She shrugged her shoulders composed herself like nothing had happened, got up and just walked away, only to come back a few moments later and tell me that she wanted me to actually shock the rings the next time.

That, my friends, is a woman with a fucking huge set of brass balls hidden up somewhere amongst the chrome plated piercings and a kink factor that pegs off the beaten path.

Tanner Nut Tasing

It never fails to amuse me, how the direct powers of peer pressure and alcohol have the ability to make people do dumb shit. Case in point my boy Tanner here. He is your normal Key West type resident who survives working in the hospitality industry and drinking until the wee hours of the morning; getting up and doing it all over again. We met though mutual friends and then of he became a part of the late night drunken downtown vampire buddy club crew.

During one of our previous meetings I was informed that he had pierced his cock. Let's just cut the shit; he was bragging about piercing his cock. As you may have read previously this isn't the first, second or even third time that I have had the opportunity to view a penis in its natural or unnatural environment. I am totally secure in my manhood and the event being kind of like the beginning of a train wreck (you just have to look).

So I told him, "You rammed a nail through your dick? Whip it out, let me see it." Instead of fuck nugget doing the manly thing, and stepping up to the plate and whipping out his freshly pierced meat stick for all to see, our boy whipped out his cell and showed me the pictures of what he told me was his freshly pierced cock. Oh no buddy. I call bullshit. As you can tell, I was not impressed, but I knew he was going to be a future victim. Uhh, I mean recruit in the fine game of Shock the Monkey.

Now you may ask, how does one convince someone to place electrical current directly upon their genitalia? This is a two part answer. First, some people are just fucked up, uhh, I mean adventurous, and will do it just because, and they need no convincing at all. For all others, you incorporate those people in the plan A portion. The ones like Madam H, or other females, like the hot little waitress sweet Mrs. Jessica, who this fine gentlemen just happened to be hanging out with, are the answer to the how to make guys do stupid shit. They will convince the rest of the chodes, uhh, I mean recruits to do your bidding, by using the fine art of peer pressure.

Side Note: One girl will work better than ten guys in circumstances such as this one, especially if it is a guy that you are targeting; you know, tell them that they are not tough enough, strong enough, or good enough. Or, you can resort to old fashioned name calling. Males are more susceptible to this tactic than females; especially if you combine the name calling with the use of some sort of alcoholic beverage as leverage to help them stroll so effortlessly down the path of the enlightened. This was Tanners case.

On this particular night, Tanner came to me and was telling me some bullshit filled with manly bravado. Not missing a beat I presented him with the challenge of a life time. I told him that he had to be tougher then the girl who allowed me to give her direct vaginal shocking to her pierced vagina. He had to be a lot tougher then that girl. Question a mother-fuckers manhood, add liquor, and they will rise to the occasion, as did this recruit.

So it being very late in the evening and the staff and I were in desperate need of entertainment, I closed down the back half of the club to all but a select crew of employees and friends of the freak show. I then handed him the ritualistic shot of love, told him that if he completed this mission I would no longer call him a pussy. That, my friends, is what sealed the deal.

So now our little recruit is by the back stage, he has his pants zipper open and for some unexplained reason he is vigorously squeezing the hell out of his nuts, which in my opinion looked more painful than the event that was about to take place. He began to be very dramatic doing what I can only describe as the ancient dance of the ball holding nut grabber. He was hyper ventilating and after about ten minutes of pomp and circumstance he told me that he was ready.

Thank fucking God! I could feel myself getting older. I snapped the black rubber surgical gloves over my hands for added effect and pushed the trigger button which let off the light show. I added a little pressure and immediately 650 volts made contact with his nuts. The electricity coursed though his body at near the speed of light if not the speed of sound. He fell to the ground in the fetal position, wriggling in pain like a donkey kicked him in the balls. Small donkey incased in the form of an electrical stun gun. Outcome— still the same.

Dick Waving Gone Wild

It would seem that I was visited by one of the Four Cocks-men of the Apocalypse tonight. I should have seen the signs, feebly, weebly, wobbly, fat and drooling on himself. Add to this equation that I was told to "fuck off," because I would not give him a cash advance on his credit card. I did that mostly because he was too drunk and couldn't sign his name, but after the, "fuck off" statement he wasn't getting shit but directions to the door. As they said in Animal House, "Fat, dumb, and stupid is no way to go through life, son."

Somehow he was able to convince me that he could get more money out of the inoperative cash machine. So, butt nugget got a hall pass. For Christ's sake, I wouldn't be doing my job properly if I didn't help him empty his bank account, especially after that harsh, "fuck off" statement he made to me earlier. How would I be able to look at myself in the mirror in the morning if I didn't at least attempt to help this poor bastard out of the rest of his money prior to throwing him out the door?

Later that evening I see him holding on to the corner of my bar, and prior to Suzie Q and me just laughing in his face, we watched him for a moment to see what he was doing or going to do. He placed his head on the bar, mostly because he could not stand up. Then he looked directly at me and I noticed a little gleam in his eye. It was the gleam of I have to puke, shit, piss, or throw up, but I'm not sure which one will come first. I pay close attention to people's body language and indicators such as these, mostly because I'm the closest but most of the time I'm the guy who's going to have to clean that shit up. Needless to say, I'm not down with that.

I watched his hands go down towards his trousers and start to fumble around a bit. So I decided to walk around the bar to see exactly what the fuck is happening. Knowing drunken guys, and how drunken guys think, I'm thinking that this ass clown is going to attempt to piss at my bar. I'm thinking—seriously? So I walk around to the front of the bar and notice that dipshit has his pants open exposing a pubic mound that resembled Buck Wheat in a leg lock. His pants were hanging off his ass. If ye ole butt nugget had a cock it was very, very small and nestled in his thick ass jew-fro of a man bush that was protruding from his unzipped pants. No man-scaping here boys and girls.

Anyway, now our half naked drunk munchkin has noticed me standing over him, and gives me a shit eating grin again. You guessed it, I pull out my taser and palmed it to make it more concealed, and I tell him that he has to holster his man business, zip up his shit and get the fuck out of Dodge via the nearest exit available as I'm pointing to the exit sign over the nearest door.
Cock knocker looks at me and says, "Or what?"
In order to help him visualize the next chain of uncomfortable events in his future, I took the hand that concealed the taser, put it in the general area of his nut sack and let that puppy bark.

Note: A taser, like a shotgun has a unique report. It's a sound that once you have heard it you will never forget it. Add to that, the light show of arcing, sparking, and lightning bolts that makes even the strongest of men cringe in fear and you will know exactly what it is even in the most severe drunken state, ZZZZZZZZZZZZZZZTRTTRTTT!!!!!

Our boy immediately woke the fuck up as he saw lightning bolts seemingly coming from my five little fingers in the general direction of his ball sack. In the quickest most sobering fashion he holstered his junk, zipped his shit and informed me that he was very, very, sorry and would be leaving right now. He made a direct bee line for the brightly marked exit sign and left the area. No, piss, shit, vomit, blood, guts, or anything else on the floor of my bar to clean up, I would say, mission accomplished.

Karma is a Mother Fucker

Seldom does one get the chance to see Karma literally drive by and ass rape someone who really needs it. But I'll tell you that at certain times, Karma seems to love me. It has provided me the opportunity on several occasions to witness these lovely events.

So this little gem starts out like this. Here I am minding my own business at work when one of my girls (Melina) comes to me and tells me that she is having some personal issues, and needs to leave. I asked what the problem is, but for some reason she was not willing to tell me. Since that is the case I take a look around, monitor the crowd and tell her to take a break and come back in an hour because I can't let her go just yet without her giving me some kind of logical explanation as to what fucking tragedy or personal issues just caused her world to come crashing down in rapid fire succession.

Why or what would cause me to allow her to shag ass, and just leave? No tears, no crying, no tugging of the heart strings, means NO/GO.

So time went by and the clock ticked away and as the pre-described hour came to hand and so did my wayward stripper, asking to leave and, of course bringing on the water works this time. Hell, it was slow. What the fuck. I didn't have anything to lose, her house was paid and unlike the song (A Lap Dance is Better When the Stripper is Crying), I'm here to tell you it's not. So I tell her pack her shit and shag ass. I get the standard euro kiss, kiss, hug, hug as her ass is leaving through the back door. It wasn't three minutes and I hear someone knocking. I open the door to find another one of my girls who is saying that Melina is having a problem with some guy in the middle of the street. So I take my big ass outside in the middle of the street and notice some ass hat screaming at Melena and that she is still crying.

I asked her, "What the hell just happened?"
She told me, "This mother fucker just ran over me with his bicycle." She then began to show me red scrape marks and residual tire tred on the back of her legs as she is wiping tears away. I turn my attention to the thug life poster child with the bicycle who (of course) was dressed appropriately to fit the part. You know he had his pants hanging way below his butt cheeks, belt around his thighs, and his hat flattened sideways. As you may be able to tell I'm already not impressed with the situation. But wait there's more.

Shit bag is now yelling at me exclaiming, "Yeah I hit that bitch with my bike and I'm going to do it again. What the fuck is she going to do about it, cry?"

Apparently our vertically challenged friend was also having a vision problem that night. I only say this because he did not hesitate one second while looking at my 6'4" 330 lbs of ass, towering over him, and standing directly between him and his victim.

Gentle readers two can play this game. Fortunately it's a game that I am really familiar with. I know all the rules, not to mention I like it. So it looks like it's my turn. I unleash a verbal barrage of fouls and filth on him that would make a drill sergeant proud. I mother fuck this dirt bag prick up one side of his sagging pants and down the other like it's going out of style.

When I was done with my diatribe Captain Corn-hole attempted to inform me that he was not scared of me and then picked up his bike and attempted to hit me with the fucking thing. What in the seven levels of hell is this about?

I catch the bike in mid-flight, applying direct pressure upon it, causing it to move back into the general direction of my drunken stripper battering illegal alien friend. Amusingly enough, he seemed to have an allergic reaction of some sort. I'm not a scientist but my hypothesis would be that his current ailment was probably due to a combination of the force of gravity, and the weight of his bicycle coming back at him at a faster rate than it was launched. Or maybe his pants that seemed to be hanging off his ass cheeks, bound up his legs from moving and steadying his drunken ass in the vertical position on the planet causing him to make a tragic and violent impact with the ground.

I felt it was my duty to attempt to communicate with this sky crane in words that he could readily identify and understand (you get it; I started cussing his ass out again). I then see a band of drum banging hippies appear out of nowhere. I'm thinking to myself, who rubbed the hippie lamp and let these assholes out of the bottle? The lead hippie is some non shaven, drunk ass, rainbow tie die shirt wearing, fucktard, claiming that he has seen everything. He is asking me why I'm attempting to steal this poor man's bike. Then he continued to tell me that I should give it back to him immediately. He then followed up with his closing statement, "Stop picking on him, and let him go."

I looked at my granola eating friend, and asked where the fuck he was about three minutes ago? You know when this dip shit here hit the girl with this bike, and then attempted to hit me with the same fucking bike?

Bongo boy called me a liar, and then in the best Scooby Doo, Shaggy back street stoner lawyer talk, added some democrat bullshit about how none of this was his fault, while being dramatic and pointing to the guy on the ground. He was a product of his environment and it was all a misunderstanding.

He never hit anyone and I was obviously being oppressive towards this guy. Apparently this, combined with the previously mentioned Mexican national hitting me with the bike pegged my bullshit meter. I was forced to pull out my can of Hippie Be Gone, more commonly known as pepper spray, and pointed it in my new found tree hugging friend's general direction and calmly told him to get the fuck away from me. I then advised him that if he wanted to do something productive he should find a functional cell phone and call the cops. Amazing how this shit works, just mention the word cops and let me tell you, all you will see is a flock of scattering hippies with a case of get the fuck out of Dodge syndrome.

The gods of war must have been happy because I noticed a K.W.P.D. officer approaching from the area of Duval Street. He arrives at my location and nonchalantly asked what happened? As I begin to tell him my side of the story, Bongo Boy comes bouncing out of the woodwork again proclaiming to all who would listen that he has seen everything. He gets back to the crime scene smelling like bad skunk weed, a dirty diaper, and burnt hair.

This is when the cop says, "You have an ID?"

To which the red eyed hippie says, "No, why do I need an ID?"

The cop replies, "Because I'm going to need to know what name to put on the arrest report when I search you and find all those drugs you've been smoking."

This strikes home with my hairy, vegan buddy and once again discretion seems to be the better part of valor and he shags ass off into the woodwork never to be seen again.

Finally, I'm allowed to finish my synopsis of the events that unfolded. I showed the nice officer the proof of battery to the victim, told him my side of the story and allowed the fun to begin. When the fine officer attempted to talk to our drunken, bike swinging bandito, A.K.A. the suspect, he said that he didn't speaky de english. This is typical in cases like this. So I added my two cents worth. It would seem that amnesia has set in, because about ten minutes ago he was making the speak-O of the lingo just fine O. Am I to believe that you were was having some sort of religious experience and speaking in tongues? Maybe you were possessed by the Devil? Just for the record, I'll quote to the fine officer exactly what you did say, which can of course be verified by the victim, just in case you have forgotten, we were both here.

It went something like, "Yeah I hit that stripper bitch with a bike, and I'll do it again! What's she going to do cry?" That was just prior to your face making contact with the pavement because you attempted to hit me with your bicycle too.

It always amuses me how something so simple can bring back memories and the ability to speak the language. My little friend started a rant directed to the fine police officer. I was mildly amused as the verbal diarrhea spewed forth from our drunken dip dunks, cock holster in great abundance, and amusingly enough in recognizable English.

In the time it took me to hit the office and type up a witness statement about our little friend, he apparently dug himself a hole to a depth that he would not be able to crawl out of. It would seem that during his rant he waived his right to remain silent as it passed by several times. His ability to obey legal directions was hampered by who knows what kind of substance that seemed to be clouding his brain, and he was irritated to the point that he now wanted to cause the nice police officer some sort of harm or bodily injury.

Note to self: Gentle reader, cops in any state do not like to be accosted by drunken Mexican nationals, or any other drunks for that matter. So our boy gets a taste of the ever so popular, "Don't Taze me Bro," syndrome.

This would be the point where Karma comes back around ass rapes our little friend and gives him one hell of a donkey punch in his man business. Apparently Karma's not done yet, on the way out the door karma shits on his best clean sheets and wipes its Karmic ass on his favorite curtains, then for good measure lights the room on fire prior to slamming the door in poor old Pablo's face.

Needless to say our boy took approximately 30 seconds of ride the lightning action from one of those new fancy taser pistols. Apparently, he was not listening to the loud repetitive verbal commands given by officer friendly, "To stop resisting."

Normally people being tazed will bring on a whole case of act right. Did our little friend learn his lesson? No! He continued to want to cause a ruckus. The technical or legal term for that would be known as resisting arrest, which, of course, gave him more attention in the form of added bonus materials including the use of hobble devises, spit masks, concluding with a nice ride to the county jail and a cool seat in the chair silence. Our rocket scientist's' charges went from drunk and disorderly conduct, and simple battery, both of which are misdemeanors' to full blown felony battery on a L.E.O. or Law enforcement Officer.

Just happy I can do my part keeping America clean, teaching useful English to the uneducated and keeping little thug wannbe's off the street.

The Birth of Five Hour Energy

As the saying goes, "I've been around the world, twice met everyone once, seen two white whales screw, and watched a monkey fuck a football". I have seen a lot of things, but I never seen nothing like this before. Girls putting things in their snatches, or other orifices for some reason is not an uncommon occurrence around me. Now, I'm not complaining at all, not even a little bit. Boys and girls I believe I have seen a little bit of everything: butt plugs, beer bottles, coke cans, dildos, vibrators, fingers, fists, a football, and one Five Hour Energy drink bottle. For all those in shock at the current writings I have to tell you a vagina is a wonderful invention given to us by the Gods. As most guys know its user friendly, and resilient. It can take hours of abuse and still snap back to its original shape and form almost immediately. If you don't believe that, look up any child birth video on YouTube; proof positive that a pussy will stretch a mile before it rips an inch. All you fellows thinking that your beating up the box.. Think again.

Well our little bartender Becka had a habit of slamming Five Hour Energy and chasing it with a Red Bull every couple of hours. That in itself was amusing to watch her bouncing off the walls, slinging drinks, pouring cocktails, and slamming the money in the cash register like a crazed crack head. Watching this unfold is nothing less than a pocket full of pure awesome.

So on one particularly slow night I was bored and concocted up a really bad idea. I took one of her Red Bulls and Five Hour Energy and convinced one of my girls (Madam H) to reenact their birth and let me video tape it. Apparently she was bored also, because she agreed almost immediately. Well folks, for some reason we had technical difficulties with the can of Red Bull. Due to sharp edges on the can, no curves or something it just wouldn't go in. Self admittedly on Madam H's behalf, she told me that she had put bigger thing up there before. So, we can safely say it wasn't for lack of trying on her part.

So we moved on to something a little more maneuverable. Presto Chango! Madam H regained her composure, got a second wind did what she needed to do, to boost that little bottle up, up, and away inside of herself. As she held it in, I prepared the lighting, and focused the camera in the general area of the drop zone. You know, so I could get the best video footage possible. She held it in and counted to three, pushed out and reenacted the birth of a little Five Hour Energy bottle. It just dropped out hitting the stage, bouncing twice and rolled into the corner. All of this action was fabulously caught on a very clear, up close and personal, videotape which I still have to this day.

So, during the next scheduled feeding frenzy and induction of massive amounts of energy drinks, I popped on over and showed Becka the brand-new hot off the press video. The look of shock and awe on her face was priceless.

I believe her statement was, "I'll never drink Five Hour Energy again."

And my reply was, "And you'll never look at one the same way again either."

Door Kicker Guy

This butt pirate, who said that he was a law student from the University of Who Gives a Fuck, apparently gave $300 bucks to a stripper named Anna, to do who knows what? Let the record show that whatever our wannabe lawyer wanted done never happened and now he is demanding a refund from me. I attempt to explain to him that not only do I not have a stripper named Anna, but since your ass is a law student you should know that prostitution is illegal in the state of Florida, amusingly enough and obviously unannounced to you, you actually did get fucked.

I will agree the circumstances of this event were probably not what you had envisioned, but none the less kind sir, you've been fucked good and proper. Now as you can see we are closed for business. Once your hangover goes away and the sun rises and falls a brand new day will be upon us, and you will be allowed to re-enter the Boner Ballroom and try your luck once more, but I will warn you, I sell three things on my menu.

Ladies and gentlemen please repeat the mantra of what we actually get in a strip club?
1, Drunk,
2, Horny,
3, Broke.
And for the bonus, remember there's NO sex in the champagne room.

I showed our newly acquired friend to the door and closed it abruptly. It would seem this did not sit well because now this boy is standing outside kicking the shit out of my door, not only did he kick the side door, he also went to the front door and kicked that one, too. Then a little further down the street in the front of the pizza shop and continued his door kicking frenzy. I'll just say, if it was a reaction he wanted. He got it.

Prior to him doing any more damage to any of the buildings, our security staff surrounded him, and called me on the radio. I came to the front, detained our subject with a fine pare of custom fitted, chrome plated bracelets, otherwise known as handcuffs, then inquired as to what his problem was? At that point it would seem that he did not want to have a rational conversation. No problem. We casually waited for the police to arrive on scene while our friend verbally berated everyone in the general vicinity apparently just for the sake of hearing his own mouth rattle. When the Police finally arrived, our counselor in training attempted to inform them that he knew his rights. He was the victim and wanted to press charges on us for battery and kidnapping. To my recollection he didn't mention the hooker thing, but I did. I also took the liberty of pointing to all the damage of several doors, windows, and broken wood in the area that all seemed to have shoe prints that matched his exactly. He was subsequently arrested for solicitation of prostitution, attempted burglary, criminal mischief, battery, and resisting arrest.

I'm not sure if he ever got the lawyer job he was talking about. All I can say is if you're going to be stupid, you better be tough. In the grand scheme of things he was just another dip shit who arrived on vacation, left on probation. The island just gave him a taste of what it's capable of.

Other Notes: Cops usually don't give a rats ass what you do for a living, but when you're being arrested, and you tell the nice police officer that you are a lawyer or a law student it defiantly adds humor to the arrest report because for some reason they always add that part in.

Amateurs and Fat Girls

It never ceased to amaze me all the amateurs who went from prude to pole worker within a shot or two. I would have women of all ages come in with their boyfriends, husbands, watch the show for awhile and then automatically think that they could do the same things the dancers did on stage.

The first step is always pound down the liquid courage; ask to get on stage to spin around on the pole. Some of the women wanted to impress their boyfriends, others wanted to piss them off. A select few more just wanted to live out a fantasy of being on stage and swing on the pole. That in itself was always amusing and never worked out for the amateur as they thought it would. The truth of the matter is it's hard to do proper pole work on the stage. Some of my girls

127

made it look so effortless to the point that anyone would think they could do it. You could always tell the new girls trying to get a routine down by the bruises on her arms and leg.

Either way it was a win/win for me. The rules were basically the same. You get on the stage; you're going to get naked. All participants were informed of expectations prior to getting on the stage. Secondly there was a fantasy fulfillment fee that was to be paid to the dancer from the proceeds of the stage set that was originally slotted for the spot on stage. Simply put, if you were going to take her stage time, you were going to pay her for it. Some of my girls didn't mind as much as others did. At the end of the day it worked out. The guys got to see an amateur, my dancers got to take some amateurs clothes off and collect the proceeds from the impromptu girl on girl liquid lesbian stage set.

For some reason guys always love the amateur show. I think it's just the thought of maybe seeing the girl next door topless or even better bottomless that brought the customers with cash to spend and money to burn to the front row. It was happening so frequently for a while I even ran an amateur night. When we were really slow I would assign an amateur a dancer for the evening who would attempt to teach her all the pole moves. Who better to learn it from than a professional?

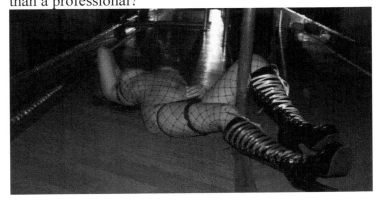

Bitch Catches Her Hair on Fire

I'm here to clear up the air a little bit, and help out a lot of you gentle readers who may not know about things such as this. So here it is. What are the three things that you're going to get when you go to a strip club? Do I really have to say it again? You all have heard it before. Drunk, Horney, & Broke; not necessarily in that order.

You will be plussed up before the book ends. It always amuses me when I hear guys coming in talking shit about how they're going to get lucky and leave with a stripper, but when the women come in, two things usually happen. The first thing that usually happens is they let their inner slut come out wanting to be on stage, or on the pole.

Number two, the catty bitches always start talking shit about all the dancers in the club. The normal rhetoric is stuff like "look at these ugly whores." knowing damn good and well that they couldn't get their sea donky asses on the stage on their best day because motherfuckers would throw rocks at them.

Pretty standard jealousy shit really. Being a dancer is such a rough stereotype to shake. In actuality a good Stripper always exudes the illusion of availability but never really is. It's just like Chris Rock says, "There's NO sex in the champagne room. NONE!"

So this brings several stories to the top of the list but the most memorable would be when a group of people walked into the club and right off the bat, I knew there was going to be an issue because of the way the woman in the group was acting. The guys went directly to the bar, ordered some drinks and found a table close to the stage. The boys started having some fun. They ordered a couple of shots, slammed a beer or two and were tipping the girls, laughing, joking, and so on. You know the stuff that you're supposed to do when in a strip club.

Apparently, this did not sit well with the girlfriend. And it goes to show you that you just can't fix stupid in some people. Note to self, if you already know that your girlfriend is a psycho, maybe it would be best to leave her at home when you plan a little event like this. Seriously! you know she's going to be mad anyway you might as well have a good time while your out.

Allow me to provide you a brief description of our girl. Of course, she was a little uhhhh, a little chubby, about a hair shy of 250 lbs. I know, according to most people's standards a 250 lb woman is more than a little chubby, but I was being nice. From the looks of her, she has not had anything that resembled game for about 10 years.

I could see how she might be a little bit intimidated by her surroundings. She was hispanic type, big hair, big earrings, big everything and rocking a mad F.U.P.A. What's a F.U.P.A.? Fucked Up Pouch Action, or according to the fine people of the Urban Dictionary, an acronym for, "Fat Upper Pubic Area"; common misinterpretations include: "Fat Upper Pussy Area," "Fat Upper Penile Area," descriptive of the phenomenon common with men and women so afflicted by obesity that their pubic area is used to store patches of fatty waste. You see them everywhere. Unfortunately, it's common in this day and age.

Now this woman's FUPA is something you would expect a baby kangaroo to jump out of. That being said, of course she is talking shit about every one of my dancers, every chance she can get. Unfortunately she is making her opinion heard not only by me, but everyone else in the club. I'm thinking to myself, you fat ass Jaba-the-hut looking, 10 sandwich eating bitch! You need a mirror; and might I suggest one of those big wide angle mother fuckers so you get a good look at yourself prior to casting judgment on anybody in here. It would seem that some people are just unable to have a good time, and she is obviously one of them.

Amusingly enough, her little diatribe was to be short lived at best. During one of her head bobbing, chicken necking, negative Nancy rants, our girlfriend was waiving her greasy hair and just happened to have it land, extensions and all in a lit candle that was on the table for ambiance. The good news is she was sitting in front of one of the smoke eaters in the club. This thing is supposed to recycle the air; you know, out with the bad, in with the good. But I can tell you that this particular piece of machinery hasn't worked in well, never. It has never worked the whole time I've been at this club. Not once, not ever! Anyway, as I sit and watch as her hair catches aflame she is still in mid rant and totally unaware of what is happening. I see the flames rising and being sucked into the smoke eater. This suint pronounced C U N T, is starting to look like Michael Jackson in a Pepsi commercial. Her boyfriend notices the problem and wants to add a shot of Bacardi to the party.

This would not only add insult to injury, but increase the burn scale at the hospital. So against my better judgment I had to intervene and stop him. A couple of his friends started beating her in the head attempting to smother the now rising flames. A dancer came by and poured a bottle of water on her face and simultaneously of my bartenders is hosing her down with the soda gun from across the room.

You can't make this shit up.

I think the funniest part about it was that she didn't have a clue as to what, or why any of this was happening. One minute she is talking shit. The next, four people are screaming at her like a troop of raped apes, beating her about the face, head, neck, and breast area attempting to put out the three alarm fire burning through her nappy weave, and delivering a giant case of shut the fuck up at the same time. Situation is handled. Tragedy is averted. The Screaming Alpha fire has now been contained and downgraded to smoldering ashes of stinking burnt hair, and melted weave which has fallen off her head and is now being drug across the bar room floor attached to a dancers shoe.

Due to the shear embarrassment of the situation, she quickly and quietly removed herself from the premises never to be seen again. On a lighter note; it would seem that Karma has come full circle once again.

The lesson here is, if you can't have a good time, stay home.

Switching Teams

    I'm always amused when I get a smoking hot dancer that I know partakes in the pussy. Meaning that she is a full tilt lesbian or very, very bisexual and then for whatever reason wants to switch teams. This is when they usually come to me and say something like, "I don't know what it is, I can't find a guy to fuck me?"

This is when I just stare at them and say something like, "You do realize that I am a man right? Due to my training and experience in this area I have to tell you that's bullshit. You darling own the pussy. F.Y.I. That little box you have if used correctly has the power to run the world and you're working in a strip club. You have noticed how many men come in here and pay you good money just to take a look at it right? If it would just so happen that you wanted to give a little of that pussy away there wouldn't be a problem finding a willing recipient. Some poor bastard would really be willing to fulfill his fantasy of taking a dancer home tonight and getting into some action. All you have to do is pick the lucky guy."

I've seen this same scenario unfold several times in the past, and I have heard more than my share of girls make outlandish statements such as the previous one and all I can say is, "You're not really trying, or you're being really picky."

So after about a week of listening to this rhetoric I asked my little dancer friend, we will just call her Jewell, "What do you like in a woman, what do you think you like in a man, and most importantly why are you thinking of switching teams?" I really wanted to know why she wanted to change horses in midstream so to speak. "I noticed that you have always hooked up with girls that look a lot like dudes. Now why the sudden switch to uhh dudes?"

She told me that she didn't know, but she always liked androgynous looking girls. Definition: girls who look like dudes. Now I'm not sure what the point is there but hey I'm game to at least listen. I figure that we had something in common. (or at least we used to, we both liked girls.) So I'm here to help a sister out if I can. And it's in the job description I think.

So here I am thinking, if I was a woman into girls, I would hope to God I would at least be a lipstick lesbian and hooking up with good looking girls. But, I also know that there is someone for everyone and now for unknown reasons my little girlfriend wants a man and has told me so. Hey variety is the spice of life I guess.

This brings us up to speed. Fast forward a week and our girl Jewell comes into the club with a group of people two girls and two guys. They walk on up to the bar and Jewell comes up to me and asks "Well, what do you think?"

I say, "About what?"

She says, "My date."

To which I respond, "Oh, you're still trying to get laid by a dude right? That is not the guy you want, he's obviously gay." She legitimately seemed surprised. So I continue to add, "Look at him, king metro-sexual, he's just what you're looking for in a woman. He is kind of androgynous. He could go either way. Put his ass in a dress, some makeup and a wig, slap him on the ass and call him Suzie. Hell, he would pass for a pretty bitch in the drag show."

That's when metro boy spoke. He said something like "Yeahh, Ummm, I'm from South Beach and I just LOOOOVVE the whole Key West vibe; the ambiance of the Keys is great. Everything here is so laid back."

As I attempted to hold my laughter down to a mild roar Jewell rolled her eyes at me. I said, "Well that's an indicator. Have you ever known a straight guy say shit like that? Not ever."

Jewell apparently still did not believe me. I asked how she could not have noticed this already. She informed me that he was her friend's brother, and she had set them up; to which I responded, "You mean your friend's sister?"

Jewell then gave me a manly ass punch and went back to her group of newfound friends. In a continued attempt to prove me wrong she said, "Watch this," and went to the stage. Jewell hopped on stage and started to do a very seductive strip tease. It took a little while for her new found companion to even notice that she was gone and getting naked on the stage. So I walked over to her location and acted like I was straightening the chairs at the stage.

I said, "Well he didn't even notice that you were up here, that my dear would be another indicator of the GAY!!!!."

It would seem that our boy's sister then made some sort of a scene about Jewell missing from the group and being on stage which of course now got her new friends attention and he finally mustered up the nuts to go and see her at the stage. This was the first hetero thing I had seen him do all night with the exception of drinking a shot of tequila, but I know lots of women who love tequila.

As for our girl's attempt to prove me wrong she was failing miserably. Her dance continued with all sort of lustful gyrations and some awesome pole work. As she spun around the pole she accidently dropped her panties somewhere on the stage then she positioned herself in his general vicinity by hanging on the brass ceiling bars so that she had the proper foot placement, on her newfound boyfriend's shoulders and basically put her snatch in his face. We're talking the front row son and just as I had suspected, no reaction, not nothing.

Here's the straight guy talking, "Brother made it to the Promised Land, he's at the 99 yard line with three seconds on the clock and the defense took a water break. The sweet smell of success was literally on the tip of his nose. The problem was he wasn't even interested."

Jewell finished her dance, put her clothes back on and walked over to me where she immediately delivered another manly ass punch and told me to, "Stop laughing."

I said, "Look babe, I hope you can see that you have just proved my point. This guy is about as interested in pussy as an Eskimo is in an ice maker."

But no, our girl is a trooper and apparently quitting is not in her credo. Still not giving up she made one last futile attempt to prove me wrong and took the poor boy to the back private dance room.

So being the voyeur that I am, I tuned in and I watched via video surveillance cameras as she provided one of the best grind jobs in the business. It was fornication without penetration. She wasn't just grinding cock she was grinding cock like it owed her ass money. I knew that she was trying to prove a point but the look on our boys face, and lack of a hard on just drove my previous assessment home a little harder, no pun intended. Nothing! Nada! Zip! Zilch! From the view I had on the camera she would have had a better chance of raising a hard on from a corpse. As the song ended, I watched as the frustration creped in. They both stood up, I noticed the boy grab his crotch for an adjustment and just as I suspected still nothing.

It's truly amazing what you can see on these camera's. Let me tell you guys if this mother fucker was straight he would have needed a cigarette, a moist towelette, and a place to nap. The icing on the cake was directly after she gave our boy a dance some of his actual boyfriends came in the club and this is when he let his inner queen bust out.

Metro boy whipped off his shirt and started dancing for this guy in the middle of a strip bar. It was at this point that I looked at Jewell and said, "well if that's not your final indicator nothing is. I'm not saying that he has sucked a dick but he sure as hell has held one in his mouth and rolled it around a little bit."

I got the poor girl a shot of tequila to help wash down the agony of defeat and told her, "better
luck next time, happy hunting girlfriend go out and try again."

This would be the part where she told me that she couldn't believe this shit. All this and she said that she was still technically a virgin. Meaning never been with a man before. She couldn't believe what this guy was giving up. I had to remind her that Metro boy was not really a guy, he was just one of the girls.

Let's go back to the indicators.

1.) Metro sexual guy from South Beach loves the ambiance and laid back style of Key West.
2.) No reaction to naked hot woman on stage throwing USDA Grade A vagina is his face. No reaction to what looked to be a wonderful dance in the private dance room.
3.) Let us not forget the fact that he already has a boyfriend shown to us by the fact that he took his shirt off and started rubbing on this other Metro looking motherfucker while in a strip club surrounded by hot chicks and his assumed date who for a lack of a better description, was literally throwing the pussy at him and doing everything but pulling out his cock and inserting it on stage or the back room.

I finished by saying, "If you would like me to point out a real man who would have been more receptive to the aforementioned flirtatious advances and good probability of taking you home just to give your ass a righteous banging, like a screen door in a windstorm, I will be more than happy to help a sister out."

Taser Tony

To my recollection this goat fuck of a story was caused over a scheduling conflict. Tony had asked for a certain day off and our current property manager apparently had not put it on the updated schedule. I was not aware of the adjustments so I called her and asked if she was coming in to work? She informed me that she was not on the schedule as far as she knew. I told her that she was on the one that I was holding.

The GM of the complex wanted to suspend her for a no call, no show, which is normal procedure for club land. I told her that if she had a copy of the schedule showing her having the day off everything would be fine and I would remind the current GM of the issue and there would not be a problem.

Later that evening Tony showed up at the back door entrance to the entertainment complex with her boyfriend and her copy of the schedule. Apparently, for some reason the current G.M. at the time felt intimidated and called me over the radio to have both of them removed from the property. I met Tony at the door and she was screaming at the G.M. about the scheduling problem. So I attempted to quell the situation. Tony handed me her copy of the schedule and sure enough it showed that she was not on the schedule. I then took her into the office told her that I was making a copy and tomorrow I would solve the problem. The G.M. came into the office and asked what she was doing in the office. I informed him that I brought her in to make a copy of the schedule she had and was under the assumption that we were using and we would talk about it later. The G.M. then told me to remove Tony from the office and that she was still suspended. Tempers, as one might expect, started getting heated. Name calling ensued and Tony reached over and slapped the G.M. hitting him on the left side of his face. It was at that point the G.M. told her that she was fired! The shit, as they say, just got real. I physically picked Tony up and removed her from the office and I now have to tell her that after bitch slapping the G.M. of the complex there was not a lot that I could do to help her get her job back. I told her to go ahead and clean out her locker because she was going to be banned from the property for at least 30 days.

Tony collected her stuff as I talked with her boyfriend and explained the situation. Tony came back out to the side street exit of the club with all her stuff and was preparing to leave when the victim again returned. The moment Tony saw him she once again became enraged started cussing at him and kicked him in the ribs causing the victim to double over and scream, "I think that crazy bitch bruised my liver."

Approximately a week later Tony returned again with her boyfriend and I was called to the front of the property to attempt to tell them that they were still banned from the property. The boyfriend asked me if he could just get his slice of pizza and go. I said that would be fine because technically he was not banned from the property but Tony had to stay off the bricks and they had to leave directly after that.

The G.M. saw the suspect's near the front of the property and again they started exchanging vulgarities in Kung Fu Panda & drunken stripperese. The local police were called and arrived on scene. Tony still refused to leave the area as previously requested and amusingly to all onlookers, barflies, street people and other vagrant types started to chase the G.M. around the Tree Bar screaming like a banshee and in what looked like several attempts to deliver a plethora of deliberate stripper kicks to the nuts, liver, neck or whatever area that she could make contact with. The police officers warned her several times to cease and desist but Tony at this point was obviously suffering from tunnel vision and was either unable or unwilling to leave the area until her mission was completed. The responding officer warned her that he was going to tase her. Still she did not comply and continued her rampant pursuit of the fleeing G.M.

The cops taser was activated and made direct contact with Tony's back. For the uninitiated this particular device has the ability to drop a full grown man easily. Here I am thinking, what the fuck? I own a taser, use a taser and have had the taser used on me. It knocked my dick in the dirt, face flat down on the ground shaking like a fish out of water and not able to move much less form a complete sentence. Not Tony, who is a petite little lady who just weighs in at about a buck-o-five soaking wet with rocks in her pocket. Nope. She dropped down onto a knee looked in my direction and calmly said, "I guess I'm going to Canadian Disneyland."

Let me tell you, it was some spooky shit bro.

The G.M. took this opportunity to scream like a girl, "I want to press charges." While running away from the immediate area for the safety of a locked office in the back of the complex. She was then cuffed placed into a patrol car and transported to the local Jail.

Trifecta of Stupid

It's nearing the last hurrah of Spring Break and usually we are still weeding out the semi pro's from the pro's of this year's drink fest. The night was going as well as expected and then I get about 1,200 lumens of Mag-Light hit me right in my eye sockets. This, of course, grabs my attention, as it should. I noticed one of my waitresses pointing out an ass clown attempting to disrupt the ambiance of the establishment.

It started like this. Ass clown: white male, brown hair, approx 5'9" and 112 lbs. skinny fucker. Holding a drink of whisky or something similar he comes up to the bar and asks the bartender, Hope for a $500 dollar cash advance, to which, of course, Hope says, "That's fine."

Our ass clown took up residence in the waitress station. This is a no- no in the hospitality industry. It slows down productivity and freaks my little bartender Hope out. We can't have shit like that happening now can we? NO! For all the obvious reasons the waitress station is a very high volume area used obviously by the waitress to get drinks to the paying customers and for the champagne room. So you can see it's imperative that it stay open for the exclusive use of the wait staff. One would think this is common sense, right? Hope, knowing this, attempted to inform our highly impaired guest by saying, "Sweetie you're standing in the waitress station and I need you to move over a little bit so the waitresses can get in here; and to complete your transaction, I'll need a drivers license and a credit card."

I'm not sure what transpired next but this kid lost his fucking mind. He began to yell at my bartender and called her a, "Fucking CUNT!"

Now I can tell you this, I have been in this type of business for awhile and there are a couple of no, no's in the name calling game and one of the names that you should not ever, ever, ever, never, ever call a woman is CUNT. That is, if you do not want her to give you her complete and undivided attention, and it's usually in the form of planning your death or great bodily injury. Just F.Y.I., strike one.

Now enter Antonio. He just happened to be my new assistant manager in training. From previous stories you know Antonio has the ability to be an asshole and has the personality of a claw hammer. But while doing security at the door of a strip club, most of the time that is ok. He is very efficient, very professional and very thorough; which is a good thing because he alone did the work of three people at our club so I can understand when he gets a little irate at some of the clientele mostly due to the redundant stupidity in motion.

As stated. I'm training him to be my assistant manager and he has to develop some sort of couth in matters of dealing with unruly customers and generally drunk bar patrons. He looks at me like he is asking what to do. My statement to him was, "You wanted to be a manager? Manage his ass out the door."

At that point Antonio said in true ghettoeese, "Look here pimpin, your actions are unacceptable. You have a couple of choices either apologize to Hope for your indiscretions and act right or you have to leave."

I thought that this was a totally acceptable and professional response from the man in training. Ass clown looked at Antonio like he had a dick growing out of his forehead, and he said, "Fuck you nigger!" That's right, white boy dropped the "N" word and walked away from Antonio in my general direction. Strike two.

Under most circumstances this response would have elicited an ass whooping in the making. I was really surprised that Antonio didn't just drop off and punch him in the face for general purpose. Needless to say, I was impressed with his tactical restraint which at this point in his training was no small feat.

Now our boy is coming in the direction of the front bar, and I strategically place myself between him and the door blocking his entrance to the front of the club. I get his attention and say, "Hey my man it would seem that you have run into a couple of my associates and the outcome was not as desired on either of our parts. You have been asked to leave so before this little escapade gets out of control I'm going to need you to do me a favor and go out that door." No muss. No fuss, all politically correct and everything. I then pointed in the general direction of the nearest exit point from the club.

His response was not all that unexpected. He told me to "Fuck off!" Then followed that phrase closely by, "I'll go out whatever door I want, and I want to go out the front." He then attempted to shove me out of the way. That move is called battery, and didn't work out so well for him. Our fine upstanding citizen was immediately redirected and escorted out the side street exit with malice and forethought. That exit point just happened to have a marked unit from the City Police Department strategically placed outside awaiting his arrival.

What our prissy pants patron didn't know was that Hope is married to one of the detectives from KWPD. Small towns and instant Karma have the uncanny ability to run rampant in the Keys. The suspect was arrested for drunk and disorderly conduct and transported to jail. Contrary to popular opinion it's really hard to get arrested in Key West. So when some Karmic shit like this happens I just have to sit back and laugh about it.

Witty Banter with Drunks

Early one evening I was starting shift as I usually did. As per the norm I had the front stage working and I noticed a drunken customer standing at the cash machine staring into the darkness of the back part of the club. Every few moments he would drop his gaze to the chain dividing the front half of the club from the back.

As you may surmise the chain is the obvious dividing line or barrier that to a sensible person would indicate that one should not enter that the particular part of the club because of several reason.

(1) It is not set up or open for business and the staff is still setting up for the night's events.
(2) If it is open we have a special event going on that you are not on the guest list for and need an invitation to attend.

As I passed through I was asked by my blurry eyed, beard faced newfound friend. Why is this chain here? Knowing that I was about to have a lengthy interaction with Captain Obvious I gave him the Reader's Digest version. "Sir, that part of the club is not open as of yet, but if you come back in about 30 minutes we can get you back here if this is where you wish to be."

His next question, "Well what's back there?"

Of course my response to my new found friend was: "I am."

Customer: "No really?"

Me: "Really."

Customer: "Seriously?"

I then unhitched the chain stepped onto the other side of it and slapped it back into the secured position. Then I stood directly beside my counterpart, and for a brief moment we both took turns staring into the darkness. Was I seeing the same thing he was? What was not self explanatory about this situation? I see an empty stage, an empty bar with a bartender setting up for the evening's festivities, and a couple of employees and some friends of theirs attempting to slam down a coffee and a light dinner to get their motors running and prepped for the madness of the evenings events.

I guess that I just wanted to see life from his perspective for a moment while forming my next witty rebuttal. Me, "Ok you got me, I see a select group of people who aren't you, most of whom are employees, a very select group of patrons, and a monkey. And since we're talking, you know what's better than a monkey in a strip club? Not a fucking thing. If you come back in about 30 minutes I'll prove it to you."

This leads us into our next adventure, animals in the bar. We have had all manner of scaled, furred or feathered friends in this club: dogs, cats, rats, snakes, lemurs, and yes monkeys too. I can hear you asking why the hell you would have a monkey in a strip club. My Answer: because.

One of my girls, Stacey, had a pet Capuchin monkey named Max which she had adopted and basically was raising it as a small hairy screaming child. When she couldn't find a baby sitter for Max or just wanted to go out and about in Key West she would bring him around and then let him run rampant in the back bar, loosely monitored by herself and the rest of the bar staff. When it wasn't hanging from one of the rafters or stuck in a hidey hole it was usually screaming its little monkey brains out or attempting to massage your brain with its long assed monkey tongue while it was firmly attached to your face.

The thing about monkeys is, once they get their hands on you, it don't matter what you do it's not letting go until it decides it's finished with you. I know I've had Max attached to my face French kissing the hell out of me; an experience that I suggest everyone try at least once in their life. If you ever get the opportunity to experience a French kissing a Capuchin monkey named Max, just Do It.

Amusingly enough our intoxicated bearded friend, true to his word, returned within the allotted 30 minute timeframe and sat his ass down at the back bar. He immediately came in contact with Suzy Q and ordered another drink. Suzy fixed his requested concoction and placed it in front of him. He then said, "Hey that guy said there was a monkey here."

Suzy just looked at him and said, "Yeah there is," and went on to serving another customer. I could see the guys look of disgust, confusion, and bewilderment as he surveyed the area for a monkey. The whole time Max was in his little monkey carrier placed directly on the bar right next to his mama not three feet from him. He sat at the bar for a while, finished his first drink, and had Suzy replace it with a new soldier and some p-nuts.

At this point he told Suzy, "I think that guys a liar. He said there was a monkey in here," and took a long pull off his cold beverage, slammed it back on the bar, cracked a p-nut open, and popped it in his mouth.

It would seem that is what was needed to get Max's attention. He came hauling his little monkey ass out of his carrier, ran over to the guy, snatched his beer, stuck his tongue in the bottle, took a little sip, jumped up, grabbed him by the beard hair and an available ear lobe, pulled him in close and real personal like stuck his monkey tongue all the way up this guys nose.

The surprised patron was in shock. He rocked back on his bar stool in a futile attempt to create space between him and his new found friend. His eyes were crossed attempting to stare at the monkey attached to his face armor & snot locker. I know that there was no way in hell he comprehended any of it. I was sober and had a hard time figuring it out.

Max finally let go of his beard only to grab a healthy portion of the patrons nose and let out an earth shattering scream directly into his ear hole, then decided that was all that was needed, he hopped off the guys face, landed on the bar, snatched a p-nut and went back into his hutch in the corner of the bar. Our boy sat back up on the bar stool with a confused look on his face and said, "What the Fuck was that?"

Suzy calmly replied. "Oh that? That was the monkey."

Kung-Fu Carrot Top

21:30, fight in the club, (Colby) the suspect, ID'd by his New York ID, was so intoxicated that he violently threw up in the center dance room and when I say that, I mean not just threw up, more like the chick from the exorcist threw up. As one would expect he (of course) was then asked to leave the premises. While being escorted out the front of the club, it would seem that he wanted to get into an altercation with his father.

Here is where it gets funny. As they were being escorted out the front door, the suspect threatened to, "Kung-fu kick every mother fucker in the club." Then ran off around the corner and just stood there rocking back and forth. Not wanting to be the recipient of a kung-fu kick by a deranged carrot top looking mother fucker, Antonio, called me to the scene and stated that the suspect was hiding around the corner. I looked to see this guy, a shoeless, shirtless, skulking true to description carrot top looking dude, standing around the corner of the club staring back at me. I informed him that he should leave the premises.
Of course he told me to, "Go fuck myself."
I responded. "That's not an option my man."
He then said, "I'm not going anywhere." Then he clenched his fists, gnashed his teeth, started growling, and lunged toward me in what I would only describe as a threatening manner. Not wanting to be the recipient of that aforementioned kung-fu kick to the head, I pulled out my can of liquid justice (otherwise known as pepper spray), and applied a copious amount to the suspect's face, neck, head, and chest and breast area. Wouldn't you know it; the bastard actually got a nick on me. He hit me in the face (good enough for a battery charge I guess).

I grabbed the ginger prick and put him in an arm bar and let gravity take over the rest of the job. Funny thing about gravity, it's a law that you really can't break, 320 lbs of ass crashing down on this poor bastard's shoulder and pinning him to the very spot that he, only seconds before, had the opportunity to leave from. But of course, in his drunken state he ignored that opportunity as it passed him by.

A funny thing about combative drunks who tell you that they're going to kick your ass, fuck you up or any amount of ill willed shit that spews forth from some people's soup coolers; when they are in a compromised position, they always seem to get a good case of manners and the story dramatically changes. They are all of a sudden misunderstood. Or they were just kidding. You always hear this, "I didn't mean any harm," which translated means I really want to go away to some other magical place with unicorns shitting rainbows, and that doesn't have you in it. A place not as restrictive as the current face down, shoulder pinned and balls deep in pepper spray, hellfire and brimstone, stale beer, dog piss, blood and other bodily fluid miserable location that I cannot leave from now because I have a 320 lb gorilla firmly attached to my backside keeping me here while waiting for the local police to show up and transport my ass to a fucking jail cell cause I'm a walking douche nozzle.

Back to what happened. Just as predicted the suspect was lying on the ground, KWPD arrived on scene and asked what I wanted to do with the ass clown I was sitting on top of. My response was, "Arrest this red headed dipshit for battery and trespassing. He was given several opportunities to leave but didn't." He was last seen in the Key West Crime report.

Posers, Wanna-B's & Secret Squirrels

Well as luck would have it I found that guy in my bar tonight. There he was, sitting in the corner looking like the uni-bomber, black BDU pants, grey hooded USAF sweat shirt, bald head, sunglasses, waving his hands in the air in a tragic attempt to get my bartender Hope's attention. When she went over, the first thing out of his suck hole was, "Don't tell anyone, but I'm working under cover. I'm looking for a perp. Oh, get me rum & Coke!"

We've all had that typical ass hat come to the bar sit in the corner and proclaim to the world that he was somebody. You know the type. One of those posers that want to proclaim that they are special ops—secret squirrel undercover—ninjas or the tooth fairy, when in fact they usually end up being nothing more than lawn jockeys, parking lot attendants or used car salesmen. The interesting part of this story is that the other six people at that particular bar actually consisted of undercover officers, regular cops, a couple of spec ops guys and a real live practitioner of Ninjutsu.

Hope came back with the report about crazy corner guy not being the uni-bomber, but telling her that he was N.I.S. (Naval Investigative Service). I don't know what he thought it stood for, but it was his story and he was sticking to it. We all had a good laugh.

Gentle reader, I'm going to enlighten thee with knowledge from the well of wisdom. If you are in the spec/ops or undercover business, and working on a case, it's considered bad form to blow your cover the minute you get in the bar. If one does this in the real world his life expectancy in the business is limited at best, as is the case with our boy Jr. here. So we did what we usually do— nothing—except take his money. Guys like this in a bar are a dime a dozen. They come in spout off bullshit to anyone who will listen, get drunk, pass out and end up in the alley waiting for a cab or a ride from the local P.D to the Gray Bar Hotel. Their bad decisions make really good stories especially in the Key West crime report.

However, as the night went on our boy Jr. went from just sitting in the corner to bringing out tools of the trade, for example, handcuff's, showing off his gun belt and telling the wayward stripper who just happened to be listening to him at the time, how bad the hand cuffs hurt his back. Then he would lay them on the bar for a brief moment only to put them back in his pocket. As soon as he drove off one dancer because she was bored or not amused he would start the show fresh from the beginning. Note: it's easy to take a line of bullshit if it's accompanied by money. $20, $50, $100's makes the bullshit more believable and easier to swallow. After each rejection he would get up stumble around, order another drink, attempt to form a sentence, talk into the invisible microphone located in his right wrist followed closely by another feeble attempt to communicate with any of the passing dancers; which would always end up in total failure. He would then dry hump the air and proceed to stumble back to his perch, plant his ass, and tell Hope once again that he was undercover and not to tell anyone.

This went on long enough to grow weary of the show and not want to view act two, three or five. So I went over for an interview. As luck would have it, apparently I looked and acted like someone he could talk to. Wouldn't you know it, old drunken guy slapped his cuffs on the table and asked me if I knew a couple of girls, Sophie and Vicka, as they were connected with his target, Mr Stark. He wanted to interview them in order to retrieve the necessary information to locate his suspect.

I told him, "Hey Bro, if by interview you mean lap

dance I can set you up, but of course this is where you will need to dip into your Ops fund or ass pocket for $20 bucks. Then, and only then, you can interview anyone here for three minutes, and all the information you get within that timeframe will be yours. It's a small price to pay in order to locate your perp right?"

This is when Jr. went cup full-o-crazy and attempted to tell me that he would handcuff someone if necessary because he was an N.I.S. Agent. I laughed a little bit, gave him one of those undercover hug type pat downs and noticed that he had a holster on his right hip under his loose fitting pullover uni-bomber sweatshirt.

Boys and girls this is when the little hairs on the back of my neck stood up a bit. As you may be beginning to understand that's not a good thing. This guy just went from big mouth drunk to drunk delusional guy with an agenda, a rape kit, and possibly a gun in my bar. I backed up, prepped my ninja gear, monitored the situation and made that quick call to the real cops; rallied the back up, and waited for the Calvary to arrive.

While assessing the current situation I watched Jr. move from the back stage area to the front stage where he found a seat at the end of the stage. I placed my people at the exits, tasers were set to stun, and we were ready to give Jr. Jack Wagon a little ride of the lightning if necessary.

The boys from the P.D. arrived, I went to the front stage, and told the only customer that was between Jr. and myself that he had to move out. He attempted to provide a little resistance due to the naked blond on stage, but after he looked over my shoulder and saw the two uniformed officers he took the hint and jumped on the clue bus. He threw a couple of bucks on stage and boogied out of the way. I then got behind Jr., placed my hands on his arms lifted him from the chair, and escorted his ass out the side door with minimal disruption. Most of the other customers never saw anything. Apparently, they were all distracted; and it happened right in front of them. But I digress.

Anyway, once out the door I pull up his shirt exposing an empty holster. What the fuck. What kind of a douche bag carries an empty holster? In my experience, if there's a holster there is usually a gun in the general vicinity. So since he was now secure by the PD guys I told my security guys to start searching all the places that a gun could accidently hide and continued to listen to Jr. attempt to explain to the nice officers how he was an undercover N.I.S agent. Needless to say the cops were not amused with this drunkard who is still pretending to be some sort of law enforcement officer or government agent with arrest powers wearing a gun belt, cuffs and telling them that he was going to detain strippers in order to find the fictitious Mr. Stark.

This, my friends, is called kidnapping and is a crime. It was then that Jr. expanded on his undercover job. He attempted to explain to the boys in blue that he was also finding bad guys and buying drugs for the narcotics division of K.W.P.D. I guess that I laughed out loud a little bit while thinking he may have been not only buying drugs, but using some too.

Then he started naming his handlers and providing information about people actually involved in the P.D. The P.D. guy's started calling the narcotics guys and in another truth is stranger than fiction moment, found that they actually had this guy working as a C.I. (confidential informant) for Key West P.D.

I could only assume that after an event such as this one, the narcotics boys would not be happy about his performance and just like on T.V give his ass a burn notice and cut him loose because he just became a big liability; never mind the fact that he just blew his cover out of the water.

Mrs. Hope and BIGDADDY

Tattooed Sasquatch

The New Years Eve party in Key West happens mostly out on Duval street with all the rest of the amateur drinkers. First timers are toting their nice bottle of Corbel, smoking cigars, and holding on until the magical hour of midnight just to pop the cork, spray the fuck out of someone or everyone. Then take a swig and attempt to lay a smack on some lucky recipient's lips who they may or may not know.

We have a better class of asshole in the club during this time. The people usually have no date or no one to celebrate with so they want to be where they are and are willing to pay for that wonderful midnight experience and the illusion that they are the life of the party. All it takes is money, and you too can be the center of attention.

Then of course we have the drunken revilers who turn into exhibitionist. Now, they may or may not know it at the time, that is, what they are going to be doing but that is exactly what happens. Here is the meat and potatoes of this Gerry Springer type event that is about to unfold.

In walked this woman, approx 5"2', pushing a biscuit shy of 250 lbs. Now you could tell that at one time this lady was a lot skinner then her current weight because she had a back tattoo, Now I'm not sure what it actually used to be. At one time it may have looked good. When you could identify what the hell it was. Since the massive weight gain it would seem that it morphed into something totally different, and it did not improve its' looks at all.

The woman I was staring at, resembled more of a tattooed Sasquatch then a woman; She was big, hairy, and I didn't know what the hell I was looking at.

Her partner, was your average thuglet, you know the type, teardrop tattoo under his eye followed by the, I hate the world tattoo around his neck. His pants were hanging off his ass, probably because he got used to selling it in prison for a packs of cigarettes. Or he's just another retarded moron who can't figure out the proper procedure used to work a belt around his hips, and through the belt loops which of course is old school technology and helps to hold up one's pants if the need should arise.

Now we have our characters and the scene is set.

Later that evening, I was informed by one of the girls that there was a couple fucking in the back room. I checked the video camera and low and behold what did I see? Clown Boy and Sasquatchika attempting to reenact the scene from Road House. You know the one, where Patrick Swayze picks up the good doctor by the hips, lifting her skirt and pumping her ass like a chi-wow-wa on crack? Well it was not as cool as that. As stated Sasquatch weighed in at about 250 lbs and Clown Boy was only about 105lbs in all his glory. But that didn't stop him. No! He was attempting to get a hold of that entire ass, push this girl up on the wall and let's just say slide it in all at the same time. It would seem that the gravity of the situation was just too much for him to bear.

Now add to that scenario, me. I came across the stage to our amateur exhibitionists who were in the back room attempting to get their groove on. I hit them with 20,000 lumens of light brightening goodness from my light and that was when they both decided that they did not want to continue the show. Our boy was the first to shag ass out of the A/O; (Area of operation) apparently he lost his wood and did not like the flashlight in his face. Sasquatches' reaction was much the same. She too decided to grab her circus tent sized panties and get the fuck out of Dodge. But in her haste she apparently left her I-Phone. This friend's is a major

OOOOPS. I say this because they both left so quickly that I did not have a chance to give her the phone back. Now it's only the right thing to do, you know, to get someone's property returned to them.   First, I always attempt to call the mom, dad or the last person called on the phone to let them know where it can be retrieved. Somehow, prior to all that happening I noticed that the pictures just happen to be open. I love people. They will put all kind of shit on their phone including naked pictures of themselves doing the most obnoxious things that their mama's would be proud of...

You can learn a lot about the person who lost their phone by their pictures. Here is the disclaimer you cannot un-see things that have been seen. This of course was the case here. Not only did I find out that this girl was the daughter of what looked to be a nice Baptist family, but she was the user of several types of medications, and judging from the pictures and the locations they were taken from, I'm sure they were not prescribed to her by a doctor.

It would seem that she was also an amateur porn model of the plus, plus size. They were mostly fresh out of the shower stuff and then of course inserting large objects into her wookie-cookie; which in my professional opinion, was in desperate need of a shave. I'm sure you get the picture?

Anyway, that was when I had that eureka moment. I had her camera; I had my video surveillance and the computer. I figured that Sasquatch wanted a memory for the New Year why not give it to her? I took several of the shots of her and her little friend in the heat of the moment, picked the best of those shots and texted them to the numbers corresponding to Mom & Dad on her phone. Then I just laughed my ass off as I sat back and let the fun begin.

It was not an hour later that the couple returned and was looking for the phone.

I greeted them at the door and asked "Didn't you have to leave?" This is where Sasquatch attempted to lie to me. She told me that she had not been in the club but her friend was and he apparently lost her phone.

Antonio began to laugh and called, "Bull Shit!" So I went to the computer and invited Sasquatch over to show her the incriminating evidence, and popped in the video, threw in a couple of pictures on the monitor, you know "the ones."

I pointed out the identifying tattoo of what looked to be the map of Russia on her back, and then she knew that she could not deny it any longer. She asked if I had her phone.

I replied, "Of course I do." I then handed it over and I asked if she was interested in a DVD of the event? I told her that I could get her a copy for $19.99 if she would like. She told me yes as she walked out the door face still red from embarrassment, and as the door closed I called out, "You have a great New Year and remember it started out with a bang."

An Island Where Somebody's Come to be Nobody

"I live on an island where somebody's come to be nobody, but if in fact you were actually somebody and came to Key West, nobody would even care."

That's all me. I created that saying over the years in the bar business, and it's a total truism about the Keys lifestyle due to all the assholes who come down here thinking that they are in fact something impressive. Then they find out that it's Key West policy not to give a shit about who they are, or more importantly, who they think they are. I've met millionaires in the mangroves, billionaires on boats, and I've been on Jimmy Buffet's sea plane. I've met rock stars, wrestlers, race car drivers, actors, and country music musicians. They all put their pants on the same way as everyone else, one leg at a time.

During the wee hours of the morning (approx 03:30) I was again called to the door to quell a potential issue between a couple of "tourons" (tourist morons) who self admittedly thought that they were in fact somebody. I separated the *tourons* from the security staff and attempted to de-escalate the situation into something more manageable. So here I am talking to two twenty something year old, drunken idiots who had already been removed from the premises earlier in the evening for obviously being larger than life pains in the prostate. These young lads were laying on the poor me routine like it was going out of style. They couldn't understand why they had been accosted by the security staff, why they were thrown down the stairs, why were they choked out, removed from the property with force, and told to leave.

This of course is followed closely by the, "You don't know who we are! I'm a Division A Athlete. I'm somebody. We live in Ft. Myers. You don't know who you're fucking with. We have lots of money."

One of the X patrons pointed at his friend and said, "This guy was a quarter back for Florida State." Then continued on with, "We're white God damn it!! We're not just tourists from Minnesota" ending with, "We are going to sue you and we'll have your jobs."

Note: This Tactic seldom if ever works. I can tell you for a fact some of the people this tactic never works on. Here's the short list: cops, fireman, meter maids, and it really will not work on bar staff and bouncers. This group of people is a special brand of I don't give a fuck who you think you are!

After about ten minutes of the mindless ramblings of King Donko and his trusty butt pirate buddy Ass Lax, I grew weary of the nonsensical mutterings. I attempted to snap him into reality and see if we were in fact communicating effectively.

So I said, "Ok let me tell you what I deciphered from your sidewalk ranting, my friends. You obviously think you're someone. All a division A athlete means to me is that somewhere in lower Ft. Myers they're missing their high school prom king/captain of the two A football team and attendant of the local Quickie Mart or Slurpee Shop. Your friend here, by your own admission, was a quarterback for Florida State, and judging by his knee, it looks as if it has previously had a surgery or three on it, possibly from a football injury sustained while attending that college. I would say that his current standing with that team is limited at best, which, of course, has nothing to do with our current situation. I heard you complain of injuries, but your actions and lack of physical evidence or damage to your person, tells me a different story all together, not to mention that you both have denied the need for an ambulance or medical attention several times, and all of that has been well documented. Yet again, it looks as if you have entered into the world of, has-been somebody. Do you know what you can currently get with the phrase: You know I was a quarterback for Florida State and $1.25?? Don't worry I'll answer that for you: A frothy mocha latte from Circle fucking K, and a small one at that. Your buddy here is obviously riding on your coat tails. His future probably holds an esteemed position at Billy Bob's Tug and Rub as the back room spooge-mopper or a very bad used car salesman, and that's the good news boys. Now listen up, here's the secret, people who are somebody, rarely, if ever, have to tell anybody that they are, in fact, somebody. In my opinion if you have to tell anybody that you are somebody, you're probably really nobody at all. One of the greatest things about this little island that the both of you have invaded, is that here, everybody is somebody. And a lot of somebody's come down here just to be nobodies and that is just fine with everybody here. It does not matter if you're somebody somewhere else because as you can clearly see nobody here gives a flying fuck about either of you. If you're both suffering from some sort of withdrawals and are feeling the need to be recognized as somebody, go back north to Ft. Myers. Be somebody there. Let those people listen to your bullshit. Because frankly we have grown tired of it, and its once again time I say good night. For your own safety please try not to get choked out, fall down the stairs or piss any more people off. It could end up with your arrest by the police and by tomorrow morning everybody will know exactly who you boys are because your mug shots will have hit the internet. If that were to happen you will indeed have accomplished your mission of becoming somebody. I hope you boys officially enjoy the rest of your vacation have a nice trip back to Ft. Myers."

The moral of this little story is, sometimes, being somebody isn't all it's cracked up to be. But I was able to create this witty saying that may catch on someday:

Key West is a place where somebody's come to be nobodies and that is just fine with everybody here.

By: Chuck "BIG DADDY" Meier

It Doesn't Matter What Kind of Spices You Use; At the End of the Day an Asshole is Still an Asshole.

Not just another witty saying, it's a life lesson.

If you didn't understand the title I'll help to explain it a little better. There are times in life that you are just going to meet that one person with little dick syndrome, the one person who is pissed at the world and everyone in it, that one person who will never be happy until he pisses in everyone's cheerios.

A couple of weeks ago that is exactly what happened.

Countrified Ass Whooping

Drunks and assholes, these are the kind of people I deal with on a nightly basis. You may ask why? Pay attention. Because. I am a licensed drug dealer. Yep. We sell more liquor out of this little bar then most of the biggest bars in Florida. We are sanctioned by the state of Florida, who then collects taxes on the liquor sales, and through the kindness of their little hearts, have given my employers a piece of paper that says we can do so. So you see I was not jacking with you when I told you that I was a licensed drug dealer. I hold in my hands the elixir of life. The concoctions, cocktails, and spirits that come over the bar have the power to alter people state of mind.

How and why you may ask? Well I'll tell you how and why. Alcohol is an amplifier. That's right! If you are an asshole in normal life and you ingest copious amounts of alcohol you have no choice but to turn into a king sized asshole. In my experience it's just the way it is and that is, of course, the basis of my next ranting.

It would seem that a few weeks ago during the normal operations of the club we ran into one of the aforementioned personalities. Under normal circumstances I can talk these people out the door with a promise of future beer and a minor case of amnesia without incident. I equate that to me being a silver tongued devil blessed with the gift of gab. But if that is not enough I add that I'm blessed with the size and weight to make most people think twice about getting into an altercation with me. While working I'm always sober and possess a security staff that functions like a well oiled machine. If the situation dictates, this is something that I readily point out to my intoxicated foes who would want to fuck with the Zen and serenity of my pre-planned chaos in the strip club, and at times, or when needed, I have no problem preaching the gospel or telling a patron a bit of the good news. This usually occurs, as I'm standing with a security team.

In the words of comedian Ron White, "Look Scooter, I don't know how many of these guys it's going to take to get you out but I know how many I'm going to use." There is a lot of truth to that saying. Normally the shock and awe tactics create a moment of clarity either for the drunken patron, one of his more sober friends or family and they solve the problem for me by taking the afflicted individual away prior to an incident. I call this a winning game plan: no fight, no injuries, no arrests, no paperwork, and finally, no lawsuits.

However there is always that one guy out of every 100 or so that just feels the need to test his metal for no other reason than to do it. That is the one guy who is filled with liquid courage and you can't reason with him. This particular event started how it normally does with someone in the party taking a picture.

Why would someone do that, you may ask? Good question. I would guess on a normal level some people are just drunk and they do not realize what they are doing. However others know exactly what they are doing and want to share it with every other fuck nugget on the planet, because we are in the days of social networking, social media, cyber stalking—all that good shit. Not only is it very popular with the "in crowd," it's just easy as hell, and it seems that people are more than willing to let the whole world know where they are and what they are doing on a minute by minute basis; everything from knitting a sweater, or sipping soda, and especially sitting in the front row of a strip club face buried between mountains of mammaries.

Seriously, think about it. Some people put everything that they have done on these sites; starting from the time they get up what they are drinking, when they leave their houses, where they are going, who they are meeting and how long they are going to be gone. It's easy pickings for anyone with the proper know how to build a file on you, your friends, family, so on, so fourth, and then come rob you blind. Blah, blah, blah. That will be saved for a different book. As you see, the A.D.D. is acting up again because I took off on a tangent. Now back to the asshole.

It started off innocently enough. Jason one of my other managers and security staff noticed this lady taking pictures. He then advised her of the rules that she could not take pictures in the club. This was the turning point. The female patron stated that she would not take any more pictures but as soon as Jason turned his back our little shutter bug resumed her previous behavior and continued clickity-click-clicking away. Jason then took her camera phone away, an action that enraged the husband and this was the catalyst that released this guy's inner asshole.

Now boys and girls this asshole of whom we speak was not just your normal run of the mill asshole. No Sir! This asshole was totally amplified not only with alcohol but in my professional opinion he had a little help from the better living through modern chemistry play set, Vitamin D Ball or more commonly known as Steroids. That is, he is in an advanced stage of asshole-ism. It gives the users powers that he or she may think far exceed that of a normal asshole and graduate them to the advanced class of Suma Cum Laude and into gargantuan asshole complete with super powers.

You know the ones, "I'm fucking invincible asshole," the, "I'm going to kick everyone's ass in here starting with you" kind of asshole. They then proceed to spew forth bull shit from their lips and not only do they want to tell you, but show you, that they are knowledgeable in advanced kata and forms from karate, ninjitsu, jujitsu, grappling, tai chi and the regular old drunken knuckle style of fighting. And, that is exactly what this feller did.

Now my King Kamehameha classed asshole is pretty much on the same level as I am. Yep, we are equally matched. He is my height, my weight only drunker than a sailor on shore leave going to a Bangkok whorehouse and MAD at the world because we would not allow his wife to snap pictures in the club. I attempted to talk to him and offer some sort of resolution to our issue that did not involve violence, as I usually do; only to receive the normal drunken two fingered chest poke complete with the aforementioned threats of violence supposedly used to induce fear among lesser men. But, this also tells you a lot about my opponent. He was a blow hard pussyfied bitch or we would have been trading blows in front of the bar.

Ladies and Gents, there are people, who will talk about whooping your ass, and then there is the guy at the end of the bar who does not ever say a word, doesn't fuck with anyone, but he will walk up and just whoop your ass. Thankfully it would seem that I was dealing with the first kind. I informed him that since he poked me and that was when I let my inner nerd come out and advise him of the legal definition of battery in the state of Florida. And how his options have now changed. He should leave or go to jail. It would seem that the threat of jail wasn't even an issue. He continued to tell me that I was too old and too fat to take him on, which was amusing because we were about the same age. He then continued to tell me that he was not only going to beat my ass but also one of the other guys on the security staff. Apparently my ass whooping was just going to get him warmed up.

I usually don't engage in banter such as this (hold on— you've read the book—you know that's a lie—I live for the witty banter). Anyway, I felt the need to impress upon him that his powers of observation seemed to be lacking and that the establishment didn't just keep me around for decoration, none of this made any sense to him at all, but at the very least it was worth a try.

My main goal in a situation such as this is to get the clown out of the bar. Lucky for us it would seem that he wanted to go outside. Shit! This option looks like a win, win for me. So I gave him the good ole western gesture pointing to the door and let's head for the street. The whole time I'm deleting the pictures while following clown boy to the door. It would seem in his drunken stupor that he has lost the ability to work your everyday average door complete with handle.

What do I do? Glad you asked. Being the gentlemen that I am, I open the door for him. Now it would seem that he's still pissed. He's huffing and puffing, pounding his chest like a gorilla and then he steps off the bricks of our property on to the sidewalk which is the boundary for me. Technically my mission is accomplished. No harm, no foul, the guy is out of the club. I hand him his phone which he promptly throws to his wife, continuing to tell me how we are not done and he is still going to kick my ass. I told him that I would rather not get into an altercation, and bid his ass a good night, when all of a sudden this big fucker steps towards me and gives me a push. Well that's the second time I've been battered tonight. I have a set of rules that govern my ass when someone is attempting to hurt me.

First rule: there are no rules.

Second rule: I hit 3 ways, hard, fast, and continuously until I have convinced the opponent that he is done.

My friends this is the strategy that I have been using for years with great success, so I don't think that I'll change it anytime soon. My first strike was to Ass-zilla's throat. This affected his ability to breath and also caused his face to come into line with the next punch which I placed directly into the snot locker which erupted in a bloody fucking mess and second, caused his eyes to close which took out his vision. Third were blows to the jaw, which snapped his head in rapid fire succession to the left and back to the right. The fucker was basically unconscious when he hit the bricks.

The rest of the team subdued him and I placed him in an arm bar, so that when he came back to consciousness he couldn't resist or hurt himself or anyone else. Let's just say, it was for his own damn good. I couldn't resist telling him that he had just received an ass whooping from an OLD, FAT, one legged man, then advised the security staff to call the police and an ambulance.

Now you may think that we're done here. Not by a long shot. You see now the wife is up in arms because her prince charming just got his big ass handed to him. I informed her that she should have taken him home when she had the chance. Now if I had anything to do with the outcome of the current situation, I was going to press charges and he was going to jail to sleep it off. Apparently, this was not the course of action she was used to, because she too became enraged and began screaming, yelling and throwing blind punches in our general direction. In order to protect myself and the staff I had to take the pepper spray from my batman utility belt and informed her that if she did not stop I was going to be forced to spray her. Do you think she was fazed at all by my threat? If you said NO! You would be correct. She ran at me and another one of the security staff (Big Jeff) screaming her banshee head off. So I gave this mouthy bitch a blast of pepper spray directly in her suck hole which of course was conveniently opened due to her screaming and yelling while approaching us in a violent manner. This particular technique is now called the fiery breath mint treatment.

Her eyes got as big as saucers in disbelief of what was happening. Apparently though, it was not enough to stop her raging ass. She spit and attempted another attack which of course guaranteed her another shot of pepper spray. Once again she was anointed with the oil of Capsicum. This time I hit her in the mouth and eyes and covered her face with the orange foam substance. This one was a little better than the first shot. She wiped the spray from her eyes and rallied once more. So a third time I hosed her down with a dose of liquid justice. It was at this point that the spray finally took effect and she dropped directly to the ground into the fetal position crying, coughing, gagging, spitting, choking, puking and asking how to make the pain stop. I told her to, "Suck rocks! Stay down and I wouldn't spray her again."

It took the police a few minutes to get to the location and secure the irate patrons. I left to write the tale of woe and secured this ass hats proper place in history. I have to say that he did say one thing that impressed me while he was in police custody. His statement read, "I called that big somebitch out and he gave me a countrified ass whooping and I need to leave this fucking place before I get it again."

Lemur's in the Club

Spring is in the Air

That's right boys and girls, spring break has come and gone pretty much uneventful but still not without any of us being unscathed with the madness. Now we had our normal weirdness. Such as wet t-shirt contests, drinking down cheap liquor with lots of juice and lots of ice in big cups and people fucking in the middle of the street; but that happens on a normal basis in Key West. There are lots of testosterone induced dick measuring contests. Spoiled brats gone wild. Of these entries let me see what were the most memorable events of spring break 2011?

First I want to say that I expected more people. I'm not saying that the turnout was not impressive, but being as how the whole northern territory of the country was under a blanket of snow for umm, THE WHOLE WINTER, compounded with people getting their heads lopped off by the Drug Cartels south of the border in Mexico as if it were an Olympic sport, I was under the impression the Keys would be the logical place to go. We got our share, I just expected more. The next rant is about some of our more colorful guests.

THIRD PLACE

To date only three actually stand out. Third place goes to two people, both females, one of whom pulled her pants down on the dance floor of the club, copped a squat, and pissed all over the place. That's right, in front of God and everybody. I guess that she had to go. She was removed and left uttering the question, "What did I do??"

My response could have been, "You just made the top YouTube video for strange bitch pissing on crowded dance floor. What the fuck, were you raised by wolves?"

Sharing that spot was another girl who had apparently taken so many drugs that she was having some sort of episode in the strip club. What did she do you ask. Well, when we found little red riding hood she was all geeked out and attempting to hide under the bar. That's right, crouched down under the bar talking to herself about some invisible invader from Planet Zimm coming to get her narrow little ass.

SECOND PLACE IS MATCH BOY

This gentleman is a part of today's American society that chaps my ass. Overeducated, silver spoon sucking sky crane, who thinks that the world owes him something other than a swift kick in the ass to get him started every morning. So, here's our boy. He comes up, looks at the bartender who is facing away from him, and he grabs a pack of matches, lights one and flings it at her back. For a moment I didn't know what the hell I saw. I looked at my waitress, Jessie, and according to the disillusioned look on her face she was also as confused as I was about the general goings on. So the fuck-tard does it again. Strikes the match, it fires up and he launches it toward my bartender a second time.

Many things flutter through my mind. First, this is a special brand of asshole. Why is he attempting to light my staff on fire? What can I do to stop this odd behavior? What will have the least amount of ramifications after all is said and done?

Option 1: Take a look around and see what you have to work with. Ahhh!! I have a fire extinguisher here by my feet. How cool would it be if I hosed this snot nosed match box jockey down with a full frontal assault via fire extinguisher and then punch his ass in the mouth for good measure. This option scores high on the cool factor and would work great for movies or a real live arsonist type situation. The down side—too messy, too much clean up—it will close the bar down, be counterproductive for money making, possibly create a riot and my boss wouldn't be happy.

Option Two: Take the taser out of my holster and let him do a test drive of ride the lightning. He is attempting to either burn my bartender or catch the place on fire. I would be well within the legal guide lines for tasering his ass and it would score high in the cool factor. Problem: the boss hates tasers and he would probably just fire me so that's off the table until he actually sets something on fire.

Option Three: Talk to him and escort his obviously drunken ass to the nearest exit and tell him to not come back. This doesn't even rank on the cool factor scale; defiantly not as dramatic as the other two options, however, it is the least violent and won't cause ripples in the big pond theory.

So, I'm attempting to talk to the boy in words that he may identify with and or understand. It went something like this, "Hey fucker you probably shouldn't throw lit matches at my bartender. Knock that shit off or I'll throw you out." By now we all know me. I'm the BIG Viking looking fucker in the corner. Don't make me get up, don't yank my chain and don't poke my ass with a stick. If those rules are followed we will get along just fine.

Apparently I must have been speaking Mandarin Chinese to this dip shit because he looked at me like a hog staring at a wrist watch. He grabbed another match with his dick mittens, struck it across the box, and launched it in the same direction as the other two. Ladies and gentlemen it was at this point that it would be safe to say I lost my mind. This would be where the cool left the area. Thoughts of tasers and fire extinguishers were gone. The old saying, off with the helmet and on with the shit pot comes to mind.

Somehow I found myself operating at warp speed and in true predatory mode. I snatched this guy by the face, angled an arm around his neck, and under his chin applied just a tad bit of pressure, just enough to stop the blood flow, if any, to the fucking grey matter he considers a brain. I kicked his back leg at the knee and he fell like a limp bag of shit. I motioned to Dave to open the door and proceeded to drag his ass, caveman style, to the street where I deposited his carcass in a hole full of swill, vomit, and dog piss. At the time I couldn't think of or find a better landing spot for this upstanding citizen.

As I loosed my grip I grabbed him by the face and proceed to give him the sermon, "I don't know where you go to school now, but you should consider getting your parent's money back. Whatever your ass is attempting to learn it's not working. Don't come back." So endeth the lesson. Apparently it worked as I have not seen him since. Who says violence never solves problems.

Grape Ape

At the top of the list at Number One is the guy who threw up in the bathroom, affectionately known to the staff and clean-up crew as GRAPE APE.

I can hear you all saying: so what, someone threw up in a bar. No, NO! This one was one of those special occasions. I was informed that someone was having an issue. I told one of my security guys to check it out. He did and immediately called me to come and assist him with the issue. Upon my arrival to the bathroom it looked like a scene from the exorcist except multiplied times ten or so add purple vomit all over the walls. Yes, plural walls, and everything else, shitters, pissers and the ceiling too. How the fuck does this happen? Who does this to themselves? Goddamn amateurs. It looked as if someone stuck a live hand grenade in Grape Apes ass pulled the pin and let it rip.

My general assessment was that one of his frat buddies decided it would be a good idea to pump gallons of purple slurpies probably purchased from Fat Tuesdays down this fat guys neck hole until the realm of consciousness eluded him and he was left in a zombie like state until he was apparently trapped in the bath room and the basic body survival mechanisms just kicked in. That's right, explosive, hurling projectile vomit.

Side note: If the body is being poisoned it will go into violent reactions including puking up whatever it has decided is the poison, in this case copious amounts of purple slurpie.

Note: I understand the liver is evil and must be punished. But that bathroom never did anything to you guys. Thank you, Fat Tuesday's.

The kid came into what I like to call, a moment of clarity. This was when I got to explain to him what we wanted to happen. It's kind of like an intervention, but different. So here it goes.

I told him, "Since you are the one who is partying and can't hold your liquor, you will be the one to clean it up." To my amusement he attempted to grow a ball and tell me that it was not his fault, and he did not feel that he needed to clean anything up. Great! Obviously you're a democrat.

I said, "My friend, I think that your nuts need to sue your brains for nonsupport. Neither my associate, nor I want to clean up this shit either, since I am a fan of options; I'm going to invest your ass with two of them."

"Option number 1: You grab the mop and the bleach spread copious amounts all over the fucking, place grab the hose and clean it up yourself or we can give you option two." Our purple vomit covered friend was not a fan of option number one and wanted to know what the other option was.

I continued, "Option number two: We spread the bleach and water around and use your sweet ass to clean it up. We wipe the floors, walls and shitters with you then throw you out the door for all your silly little frat boys and girl friends to see, and show them exactly how much fun you had on spring break. Believe me, this will be a life altering moment for you, this moment will be etched in your fucking brain and you will remember it for a long, long, time to come. Just when you think you're going to be able to forget it, one of your friends will bring it up again with pictures and in living techno color."

Wouldn't you know it he grabbed the mop, bucket, and bleach then dry heaved his way through the whole cleaning process—ceilings, floors, walls and stalls. In the end, he did a good job. We escorted Barney to the door and he has not been seen since. I can only hope that he learned a lesson or checked into some kind of rehab.

Ladies and gentlemen those were the top winners for the spring break festivities. Since then I've talked to many of my coworkers and we have all come to the conclusion that the younger crowd has lost site of the original goals, they lack vision. They all seem to have a feeling of entitlement, that someone owes them something. I cannot count how many times I was told that I was going to be sued by little Johnnie's dad because he is a lawyers and we just had to let them in. But when asked what rights I actually infringed upon or which of the constitutional amendments or laws were broken no one could answer me.

My question is, "Does that shit really work anywhere else?" I would hope not but you never really know now do you.

Most importantly, I don't think that I met one kid that could handle their liquor. I'm going to breach that line in the sand and sound like an old person and maybe I am. Maybe I lack the tolerance for stupidity in abundance anymore. I'm not saying this lightly, in my time I don't believe that the goal for spring break for us as young kids was to get blind fucking drunk every night. In my mind the goal was to get laid, meet other people and explore places that we have never been before. Contrary to popular opinion, that went for the ladies as well.

It was nature at its finest, young adults attempting to have a good time. Now, our current crowd couldn't tell you if they had a good time, the zip code they were in or the planet that they were standing on. Mostly because they are in a comatose state and don't remember shit from shine-ola. How the hell are you going to get laid if you can't form a sentence? I hope you took pictures, because it's hard to be nostalgic if you can't remember any of your trip.

The Viking Horn

Shitter humor at its finest...

If you're offended by bodily functions or excretions this would be the time to opt out and go to the next chapter, but if you've made it this far congrats.

This little event happened early in my career at the club. It was one of those nights when we were busy as hell and I was doing my rounds. My boss at the time was a woman named Onnie. She told me that I had to check the bathrooms, and when I did, let's just say I was totally unprepared for what I was about to see. This is one of those times that some things that are seen cannot be un-seen. I opened the door and a man walked past me burying his head and not making eye contact. At that moment I didn't think anything of it, but then, the smell hit me like a ton of bricks. The odoriferous aroma could knock a buzzard off a shit wagon at 50 yards. I'm thinking: what the fuck is that? At first glance nothing out of the ordinary, but then I looked into the bathroom stall. There it was, the mother of all turds. Boys and girls I have seen some shit before but I have never seen any shit like this, it was so big it had its own zip code. The bowl filling description was, big, brown, and full formed; like a crap anaconda and wrapped around the total inside of the bowl twice. But that's not all. The circumference was about as big around as a beer bottle and had about six inches protruding from the water line of the toilet bowl, and proud in all its stinking glory.

As I stood there in the stench, I had a flash back about the guy that passed me in the bathroom. I could not remember anything about this guy. I mean who the hell pays attention to guys in the shitter? God, I missed out on the perfect opportunity, I wanted to fuck with this guy. Who the hell does this sort of thing? What the hell was his problem? If it wasn't him, then he knew who the hell it was. I wanted answers and one thing that I knew, was that I wasn't going to clean this shit up. Regardless of the phantom shitter's identity, either he has been locked up and blocked up for a month of Sunday's or his asshole had been stretched out like he was the pivot man in a prison gang rape scenario or maybe both.

I attempted to do the right thing and flush the Viking horn but it didn't move. The water just flowed over it. It was hardening like a block of Quickcrete. I had to tell Onnie about the gargantuan gut bomb fermenting in the men's shitter and that it was not going anywhere. She freaked out, and told me to remove it. I told her that she needed to see this thing, you know, to get a better idea of what we were dealing with. So I took Onnie into the bathroom to show off the Viking horn. She followed me into the bathroom and upon viewing this world record modern art masterpiece; she began dry heaving, and almost threw up. As she continued to hold back the gags of disgust, she screamed at me again to get rid of it.

I ask, "How would you suggest that I do that? You have a shovel, or maybe a Spatula? Let me show you something." I flushed the shitter again. Same result. The gigantic turd didn't even budge. She screamed at me once again to fix the problem threw her hands up in the air and said that she needed a drink, and left the bathroom.

I called for the cleaning guys, a gas mask, a gallon of acid, some tongs, and a shovel. The word went out over the coconut grapevine that the largest turd known to man was lodged in the strip club shitter, and I was charging admission to see it. This was not your normal turd. NO! It was something worthy of Ripley's Believe It or Not. The grapevine was correct. You wouldn't believe how many

People showed up for the viewing. I had to close the shitter down while waiting for the cleaning guy, so I started charging admission .50 cents per person to take a look at it, and a dollar to take a pictures of it. I figured if I had to stare at it, I might as well make some extra money. It was amusing the amount of people that showed up for the shit show. The turd was getting more tips then the girls on stage. In the grand scheme of things it was a win/win for me. I didn't give a shit. They could take a sample of the damn thing if they wanted to. That would make my job easier.

Bill Hoebee, a DJ friend of mine from the other strip club, came over because he heard the news and he brought his camera with him. It would seem that he has over the years been collecting pictures of poop. Apparently these little events are more common than I thought. He told me that this would make a great addition to his collection of poop pictures and still has it to this day. It's strategically placed next to the picture of another famous turd, called Big Green. Hoebee informed me that he has a whole photo album dedicated to fecal matter and this was like the holy grail of shit shots. The look on Hoebee's face was awesome. His eyes widened, his jaw dropped and his nostrils flared as he took in the sheer size and magnitude of the total mass of fecal matter. He feverishly snapped shots and we took a beer bottle to verify the size and we were impressed. It was like C.S.I. Key West except with poop.

He asked me, "What the hell dropped this deuce, Bigfoot?" I was still laughing and collecting people's money as they walked through the door. Finally, the cleaning guy showed up in full hazmat gear. Rubber gloves up to his armpits and gas mask all prepared for battle. Apparently he too has done this before. He poured a gallon of muriatic acid into the bowl and the fight began. The turd was fighting back for its life.

"The force is strong in this one," I said. It was spitting, sputtering, and had hair falling off of it and I believe we also heard a faint scream between the pops and fizzes.

The cleaning guy attempted to flush it again but his feeble attempts failed. He then took the plunger and mashed the six inches of shit still above the water line down compounding it into the bowl filling the pipes. This was classic pipe clogging poopie goodness which, of course, caused the water to rise and poop particles that were not filling the pipes to escape the bowl and land on the floor. This was a real shit storm if you will.

The cleaning guy continued on his frantic pounding of the pile of poo while Hoebee and I laughed our collective asses off. You can't beat this and you can't make this up. Shit humor at its finest. The whole event was like watching the sinking of the Titanic. But in a very different South Park meets Mr. Hanky the Christmas Poo sort of acid trip. Twenty minutes and a mop job later, the bathroom was again good to go and ready to receive customers.

The legend of the Viking horn lives on.

.

Boot Licking, Ball Kicking, Piss Drinking Good Time

Working in an environment such as this, you will run into every manner of weirdness. Then we break out the fetish guys. I'm about to tell you about a certain class of clientele that loves self-humiliation. Usually and historically speaking, guys like these are very high level types. They are heads of large companies, in charge of lots of people, have wallets full of money, and are at the very seat of power. They come in looking for a release of control or a break from their reality. Oh, and they pay well for it. It's not unheard of for these guys to spend $1,000 bucks per hour. Not only for the ass whooping, but the anonymity.

My first experience with shit like this was while working with a girl named Jerry. She was a 6'ft tall, bright red haired bombshell, with big 44 DD boobs, and an attitude to match. A real dominatrix, who came standard with the leather corsets, dog spiked dog collar, whips and chains; not to mention had some real mommy daddy issues. She just loves to beat men's asses and of course got paid to do it.

When this particular customer waltzed in, he knew exactly what he wanted and Jerry fit the bill. She, as they say, stood out in the crowd. After a few drinks and negotiations on the price, they were off to the back room. The dance started not a lot out of the ordinary—just a dude and a dancer doing what you would expect. Then it got interesting.

Jerry got up, put her boots in this guy's crotch, and applied a little pressure. Our boy started groaning and apparently asked her to step up the game a bit. Jerry smacked him a couple of times in the face, and asked if he liked it? I would say yes because the dance continued and he became a little more extreme. At one point, Jerry had this guy standing up and was kicking him square in the nuts. I'm not sure how the hell he handled the barrage of straight up field goal kicks to his junk, but he did. Adding insult to injury, Jerry then had him get on his hands and knees, slapped on the dog collar and dragged him around the floor of the club, making him lick the other dancer's boots and tipping them $20, for allowing them to do so. After the boot licking session apparently he did not perform up to par because he received a spanking for his indiscretions. This went on about 30 minutes or in dancer time 10 songs. Our boy was taken back to the private room, where he situated himself, paid Jerry the agreed fee of LOTS of money, and he was met at the door by a big black limo and drove off into the night.

This was a monthly event for a long time.

Panty Sniffers & Piss Drinkers

We also had a customer who would come in and purchase some of the girl's panties.

He said "The dirtier the better."

This particular guy was a local and had certain girls that knew what he liked and they prepared for his arrival. When they knew he was coming in they would run to the K-Mart or some other store, buy the hell out of packages of cotton panties wear them once or twice, crank out a grind job or two, then put them in a zip lock baggie and wait for him to come in.

He would come in, start his ritual by finding a nice place in the corner then open the bags one at a time, just to get a good whiff & sniff. Some people go to wine tastings, others like to sniff panties and hand the girls $10's, $20's, or $50's depending on his pallet for pussy that evening.

But just when you think it couldn't get any weirder, I have a surprise for you. After a brief drink or two he would then barter for shots of piss.

Operation Golden Flow

We had a couple of the girls who were just drunk enough to join in on the shenanigans. Money's money. They would run into the bathroom with a shot glass and fill-em up. Then they would put it on the tray of shots mixed up with the real tequila headed for our lucky customer. Yep, you heard me right. Between the shots of tequila our boy would break bad with another beverage that didn't need any additional salt. Top shelf piss comes in both forms Domestic & Imported. Both flavors at that time would go for about fifty bucks a shot.

Apparently there are even limits to piss drinking. One of the customers who took part in this activity would only request girls who drank a lot, because once he chose one of the, lets say, healthier girls who worked out, took her supplements, and all the good stuff and he couldn't handle it. He said, "It was a bit strong for him."

Dancing With a Dead Guy

Things that people take to a bar in Key West.

I've been around the world twice, talked to everyone once, but I ain't never ever seen shit like this before. I have seen patrons bring all kind of shit to the party. I have hosted birthdays, bachelor parties, and bar mitzvahs. I have had dogs, cats, birds, monkeys, and lemurs in the club but in my opinion the weirdest of the group would have to be the group of customers that brought in their dead relative. I'm not sure what they were thinking. Maybe it was the dead guys last request, but I can tell you if nothing else these guys were dedicated, whiskey bent and hell bound to have that last drink with old Uncle Randy, or whatever his name was.

That is not really the funny part. The funny part is when they leave the dead relative's remains in the bar and then the next day they have to call the entire list of bars that they can remember, to find the rum soaked remains of good Ole' Uncle Filthy McNasty.

As stated this particular group of Irishmen decided to help with one of their friends last requests by taking him on one final bar crawl prior to launching him into the great beyond. It was shots of Jamieson all around, followed by the rum drinks, chased with whiskey drinks, and gallons of beer to wash it all down. What made them fun was that they even bought dances for the dead guy in the urn. They had him in the middle of the table with $20's taped to the side.

One of the guys opened the urn and asked one of the girls if she was willing to give their friend his last blowjob. Can you imagine that? One slip, drop, or sneeze, and nothing but dusty dead guy, all over the bar? Obviously she said, "No!"

Of course I had to tell the guys that they had to put the cork back on good Ole Uncle Cletus. You know, so we wouldn't have to pick his ass up using a dust pan. Got some laughs out of the boys, but that didn't stop our group of gray haired geezers.

The beer was flowing like wine, and the money kept coming out of the wallets. Apparently, a fun time was still being had by all. They handed our girls their money and the urn. Put them all in rotation. The word spread quickly and the girls were taking turns toting the urn, back to the dance room. Every once in a while, one of the friends would wonder back to the dance room just to verify the dearly departed was getting his money's worth.

I have to say it was amusing watching girls dance for an urn full old dead guy. Creepy at best, but there was also something really cool about it, other than that it was the easiest money they made all night; no groping, grabbing, or unauthorized solicitations, lots of laughing, giggling, and carrying on. The girls all said, "He was one hell of a nice guy" (and they were making a money hand over fist). It wasn't long before the crew could no longer handle the evening's event. The old geezers started dropping off like flies and as they say the herd started thinning out. Maybe it was Metamucil time back at the ranch, or if, like most drunks, they just got shiny objected and did the drunk walk to another bar.

I'm not sure who was left in charge, but whoever it was they dropped the ball. Unfortunately, I didn't find this out until the end of the night. While closing down the ponderosa, making my final rounds, I hit all the lights, made my final walk through and there it was, the crusty, dusty urn of dead guy just sitting all upright and perky on one of the benches. It would seem that funeral party misplaced their best friend. To this day it was one of the strangest calls I got at the club. The customer actually called looking for their friend's remains. I told them fortunately his friend was right at the bar where they left him. The cleaning crew didn't know what the hell it was but due to the stylish urn, they left it on the bar by the lava lamp. Needless to say it was one hell of a last party.

Butt Sex

This story started early during the first time I worked at the club. I want to point out a disclaimer. The suspect was never arrested because the victim refused to press charges. No Victim. No crime.

There was this guy—at the time I was not sure what his name was. He was just an average, white boy, about 5 ft, 5, 150 lbs. with blond hair and worked as a local fisherman. He would make his rounds every night like clockwork. He never arrived at the bar trashed out of his mind, but by midnight, for whatever reason, he would be so drunk that he could not remember his own name. Even though the bartenders would only serve him a couple of shots and a beer to chase them down while he was there. He was always a nice guy.

Normally, there was never an issue. I just always found it weird that at midnight this kid would always lose not only his ability to speak, listen, and comprehend the English language, but couldn't maintain upward and forward movement throughout the bar.

Well, to get on with the story; one night after closing time I was busy taking out the trash. I pulled a couple of garbage cans to the back of the club, and what the hell do you think I found? A half naked white boy face down in the fetal position in the gutter with dog piss, bar swill, and broken glass. I shined my light on him; he didn't look like he was beat up, no bruises, bumps, or contusions. I did note that his pants were down around his ankles, and he had a large carrot hanging out his asshole.

I have a warped sense of humor so of course I had to laugh, I'm thinking, "What the fuck, someone threw out a perfectly good white boy." Then I looked around the alley, to
make sure I wasn't about to become the next victim of a good ole bug bunny style anal rape session. I kicked our boy, to make sure he was breathing. He let out a groan. Well, at least I knew he was breathing. I used my radio and had security call the ambulance.

I asked our boy, what the hell he was doing. More importantly why he was laying naked in my alley with a carrot in his ass? I was hoping that there was some logical explanation of this event, you know other than serial rapist. This isn't the first time, I have found naked people in the alley doing weird shit, but this was the first time I have found a guy with a large vegetable lodged in his rectum.

Our little drunk stood up, staggered around, stared at me with glazed over eyes, mumbled something unintelligible, and then he proceeded to pull this carrot from his butthole, dropped it in the alley, hoisted up his pants, and wandered off into the night.

You may think this is where this story ends, but you would be wrong. This is Key West this is where it begins.

It wasn't even a week later when our boy wandered back into the club. Later that night, surprisingly, I found the same guy, in the same position, same alley, same asshole, but probably a different carrot. Not sure what you're thinking, but I have always been told, "If it happens once, shame on you, happens twice, well you're starting to become the common denominator."

From there on out anytime he would wander in, I would announce "Butt sex in the building." It was definitely an inside joke among the staff at the bar. The customers were never sure of what the hell I was talking about.

He asked me, "Why are you calling me Butt Sex?"

I had to tell him. "Hey bro, just for your records, here's the deal. I have found you in an alley twice with a carrot in your ass. It's not even fantasy fest yet. Even if you were blacked out drunk, or you got yourself a sudden case of amnesia, you have to have some kind of a clue that something is or was wrong? I mean you bring a whole new level to the term party your ass off." This is when he got a little pissed, and called me a liar.

I couldn't believe he couldn't remember some traumatic shit like that, maybe he didn't want to, but then again, would you want to? Me neither. Just for the record, I have to say I have partied a lot, and I have been drunk more than most in my time. But I can honestly say that I have never been face down in a gutter with a carrot in my ass drunk.

We would have to watch his every move, and monitor his actions. While doing exactly this, we noticed some other guy following him around and position himself by our boy's unattended drink. I grabbed butt sex and asked him if he knew his friend?

He asked, "What friend?"

"The guy holding your drink" I said.

He told me that he didn't have any friends in here, just the girls.

It would seem that our boy made one serious mistake every time he came into the bar, he would leave his drink unattended and at the end of the night literally paid for it out the ass. You see, he had a very bad habit that turned into a pattern. He would buy a drink, leave it on the table unattended, tip the girls, come back, and continue drinking where he left off. My friends, in the world of drinking, this is a big NO, NO! No matter what bar you're at, no matter whom you are (remember this, it is important); you NEVER, EVER leave your drink unattended.

It would seem that Butt Sex was being stalked by the guy I found loitering around his beverage. So I went over and accidently spilled ol butt sexs' drink. The guy looked at me and asked why I did that?

I asked, "Was it your drink?"

"No," he answered.

"Then there's no problem. I just don't want to see anyone in the back alley with a carrot in their ass. You know what I mean?"

This guy kind of smirked and I knew something was up so I pushed this issue a bit. "Why the hell would you do that?"

He looked me dead in the eyes and said, "Straight guys won't tell on you!"

Needless to say he was ejected from the premises and since that time I have not found old Butt Sex in the back alley with vegetables lodged in any of his orifices any more. So, if you have learned nothing else from this story. Take this little tidbit of advice to heart. If you leave a drink unattended at a bar, count it as a loss. Just get yourself a new one. Believe me it's not worth the pain in the ass.

Super "V"

During my early years as a bouncer there was a guy, the stereotypical Cuban drug dealer type, or unlicensed pharmaceutical representative that came in the bar. You know the type, khaki pants, wife beater t-shirt, the chest fro kicking, big gold necklace with the crucifix of Jesus, and greased back hair. This guy was sitting at the bar and every time I walk by I would get the, "PSSST, PSSST! I got Super V!"

What the Hell is this, some third world country shit? I ignored his antics for about half the night figuring that he would just go away. But apparently the persistent bastard did not get the message.

So curiosity finally getting the best of me, and I had to ask, "What the fuck is Super V?"

It was at this point that my newfound friend and self prescribed snake oil salesman, started to explain to me not only what it was, but also the benefits of Super V, more commonly known as Viagra. He told me that this one little pill will have me performing like a teenager again.

I had to ask him, "What does that mean? To my recollection as a teenager I wasn't really that good."

Did this stop him? No. He continued with his sales pitch. "Super V will make your dick hard all night. You'll be killing the ladies."

To which I retorted, "Hey Brother, I currently don't believe that I have an issue in that department and contrary to popular opinion the ladies don't really want to be killed." Followed up by, "You may not have noticed, but my ass is 6'4" about 300 lbs. Believe me, the ladies know I have been there, and I don't believe that I have had any issues in that department. At the very least no one has ever complained. But just for sake of argument, what if you take Super V and don't hook up?"

He replied. "Oh if you don't hook up, you have to use the banana trick," and continued to explain what the banana trick actually was.

The explanation is just what you would think. First you need one banana from the grocery store, off the vine, or from a friend's house, wherever you can get one. Then you put the banana into the microwave for about 30 seconds, this should make it nice and warm, you don't want it to be too hot. Then jerk off with it until you blow your load or the erection subsides, whichever comes first.

My next question was simple, "What if that don't work?"

He said." Well, if your dick don't go down after four hours, you need to go to the hospital and the doctors will have to fix your problem, or as they say permanent damage could occur, just like it says on the commercials."

I asked, "What do you mean? What will the doctors have to do?"

He continued to explain, "They put a needle in your dick, inject you with something that makes your cock go limp, then you can start over again."

That's just wonderful. At this point I couldn't stop laughing. So I said, "My brother, you may not realize this, but if you take a quick look at my t-shirt. I run this strip club. A big part of my job is to keep dip shits like you out of here. I want you to just look around. At any time during the night there are at least ten naked women in my general area. When the wind blows, I still get a hard on, and you're here attempting to sell me something that will supposedly make my cock harder then beaver's teeth and Chinese arithmetic? Follow that up by, if I get turned down, or my girlfriend for the evening isn't in the mood, your solution to fix the problem is that I should jack off with a warm banana? And, if that solution does not work, and I have a boner for more than four hours, it could cause permanent damage to my weiner, and I would have to go to the emergency room and not only explain to the medical staff that I have been sporting wood for four hours, beat off with a banana, which, of course, is the cause of the strange residue on my meat stick, because I took your self-proclaimed super Viagra, without a prescription. And to top that off the solution is they jam a needle in my dick? That, my friend, is some shit that I do not need today."

You'll find this funny, later on that evening this guy we'll call Richard, who was apparently a customer of our acquaintance comes knocking on the door well after we closed. I opened the door to the guy, with what appeared to be a terminal erection asking about how he should fix this problem? I laughed, and told him "Maybe you should try the banana trick, if that don't work your ass needs to go to the hospital and have the E.R. staff jam a needle in your dick. Have a nice night."

Poopie Pants

Doing drugs in the club.

Contrary to popular opinion you are never going to get rid of drugs, crimes, or any other shit that people want to do. The facts are simple. People are just not comfortable in their own skin and feel that they need a little something to help them drop their inhibitions, relax, get amped up, motivated, or chilled out. Whatever the need at the time, there is a prescription that will be a solution to your problem.

I myself have an issue with drugs; I don't promote them, especially in the work place. But I know that in this line of business they will not go away. However, I can limit the amount that comes in and make it harder for dealers to sell in the club, make it harder for customers or employees to use, and I do that job pretty well.

But conversely, I'm also a drug dealer. My saving grace is the brand of drugs that I peddle just happened to be legal and I hate competition.

This next little tale of woe is how I solved an issue with a user and dealer who attempted to expand his business into my area of operation.

I was making my rounds checking things out and had to go to use the facilities. I open the door, and headed for the urinal. Unzipping my fly in preparation to take care of business and heard the sound of someone using something plastic hit the back of a toilet. Whatever it was, it made a crisp chopping noise immediately followed by a sniffing sound. Due to my training and experience, I just knew I had an asshole chopping a baggy of coke into lines, and snorting away on the back of the shitter.

Just another one of those, W.T.F moments??? So being in charge of security, and also being the nosey bastard I am. I looked over the stall. As expected a dip shit who actually worked on the other side of the complex was chopping a white powdery substance into lines and using a straw to snort the lines off the back of a dirty ass toilet tanks.

You know what I'm thinking. If you guessed I said, "What the fuck?" You would be right. The last thing I need in the club is some geeked out coke dealer freaking out and hiding in the corner. I'm only making that assumption, because the amount of coke he had was more than I would guess was for his personal use.

So I said, "Hey Bro, knock that shit off and get the Hell out of here."

To which he responded, "Fuck you! Mind your own business," then continued to snort away like the shit was going out of style.

Now, allegedly, in my past, I may have had a minor anger management problem, compounded with high testosterone that prevents me from just walking away. Back then it was more socially acceptable to whoop someone's ass that desperately needed it. Whatever the case, I had no problem with rising to the occasion and accepting a challenge from a cokehead disrespecting my authority, quick, fast, and in a hurry.

So prior to dipshit finishing his pre-chopped line, I kicked in the bathroom stall door with such force it exploded off the hinges, flying pieces and particles of wood, door handles, bolts, and my size 13 boot made contact with this douche bag. His head hit the wall, and about an eight ball worth of the white powdery substance went all over everything. It started to look a lot like Christmas in the shitter stall of the boner ballroom. The white powder was now airborne and drifting all over the bathroom. Wasting no time, I snatched dipshit up by the neck and started dragging him by his head kicking and screaming out the door.

It is at this point, dear reader, that his subconscious fight or flight response took over and decided that he needed to lighten his load so to speak. That's correct; our boy lost control of his bodily functions and shit his pants. A patron who witnessed the event unfold explained to me that as I was dragging him to the back door, there was a steady stream of shit falling out of his shorts, and landing on the floor. It was like a fucked up case of Hansel and Gretel, instead of bread crumbs he was dropping fecal matter of the large turd format all over the strip club.

I'm thinking: Shit (no pun intended)! This is great! Who the hell is going to clean that up? I should make another pass and use this ass hole to clean up his own mess, then at the very least I would get some sort of amusement out of this situation. But then I figured it would just make more a mess then it was worth.

At this point the poop was still in what I would consider evenly spaced intervals and solid in nature. So I threw Mr. Poopie Pants' limp ass, semi-conscious corpse in the alley, told him he was fired, and not to come back. He made some feeble attempt at a reply, but I had already closed the door.

A couple of hours later, our boy, Poopie Pants, who had obviously gone home and changed shirt, decided to come back using the very door he was previously ejected from.

One of the other bouncers, Alan, called me on the radio and said "Hey look Ol' Poopie pants is back." Then he told our wayward friend, "Don't you remember Chuck telling you that you can't come back? You know, after he dragged your ass out of here by your neck and threw you in the street, and fired you?"

He said "I've never been here before in my life."

Alan said, "Dude you can't pull that off. You stink and still have shit stains in your shorts. Get the fuck out."

Just another happy ending with Alan saying in his best south Park Mr. Garrison voice " Hey Ummmm Don't do drugs Ummmm k

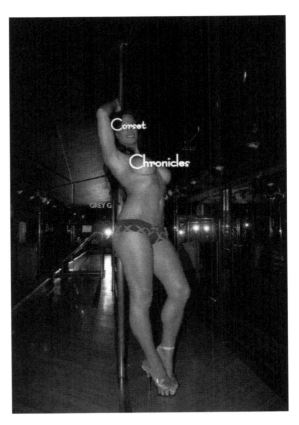

Bubbles Sayings

Bubbles is a fictitious dancer created by my wife (Dallas).

Some of the sayings have been collected over years of working in the club industry. Bubbles is not just one person, but a conglomeration of sayings that were heard at the bar, the club or in the dressing room and they all leave you shaking your head in disbelief.

My name is Bubbles and my favorite color is clear, I think that grape comes in second.

Q: Bubbles, what did you learn in college?
A: Where the Dean hides his ruler.

Q: Bubbles, what are your turn ons?
A: Uhh, long walks at construction sites, and the produce stand.

Bubbles: "I was told I shouldn't smoke cigarettes, but I don't really know what else to do with them, and I don't know why they call it smoking the cigarettes, I just suck on them."

Bubbles: "I want to get married someday, but I have to wait until I'm not single."

Bubbles: "I like climbing, that's why I live upstairs."

Q: Bubbles, do you have a fan club?
A: Yeah, I got a lot of fans; they're all three speed electric.

Bubbles: "My mom always said I should only believe half of what I hear, but she didn't tell me what half to believe."

Bubbles: "Getting an answering machine is the worst thing ever, especially when I hear the recording, 'Leave your name, your number and I'll get back to you.' Uhhh! Sounds just like most of my dates."

Bubbles: "I had to quit being a stripper because nobody recognized me with my clothes on."

Bubbles: "It's funny guys always ask me to go to bed with them, but it's always when I'm not even tired."

Bubbles: "When guys ask if I give good head? I always wonder how they knew I worked in a hair salon."

Bubbles: "I always thought men and women were equal, but I have noticed most men suck and never swallow."

Bubbles: "This guy asked me if I wanted to do a ménage a trios, but I don't do fruit drinks."

Bubbles: "A guy asked me if I wanted to do a 69 with him. I told him I didn't have a license."

Bubbles: "I was pulled over by a DUI officer. I told him I wasn't drinking. He said "I better blow a zero." I wondered how he knows what kind of guy's I date."

Q: Bubbles, why did you dye your hair Brown?
A: So I don't look so dumb.

Q: Bubbles why don't you like wearing a watch?
A: Cause I don't like time on my hands.

Bubbles: "Alimony is when you give up some sex for money right?"

Bubbles: "I can't get my hair dryer to work because apparently you have to be smarter than your equipment."

Bubbles: "I hate when I accuse someone of stealing my clothes and I still have them on."

Bubbles: "I drink water for the taste."

Bubbles: "The size of a man's wallet gauges how much I actually like a guy."

Bubbles: "I can hang on a guys every word, even if I don't know what the hell he's talking about."

Bubbles on answering a question: "I forgot, you can't hear me shake my head Yes and No."

Bubbles: "Damn, my new cell phone is broke. Never mind this is my old one."

Bubbles: "You can't say that about me. You're making it sound like I was there when I did all that."

Q: Bubbles, why are you getting Braces?
A: So my kids will inherit straight teeth.

Q: Hey Bubbles how are you?
A: I'm happy. I feel more like I do now, then I did yesterday.

Q: Bubbles you look happy.
A: Yeah, it's my birthday this month. You know I have one every year on the same day.

Bubbles on dating: "I might have to have sex with my date, but I'm not sure because he hasn't paid me yet."

Bubbles on phone sex: "I'm not sure how phone sex works; I mean who has to wear the condom?"

Bubbles commented on being a lawyer and passing the bar exam. "I don't see what the problem is, anybody can pass a silly bar exam. All you have to remember is top shelf, bottom shelf, and if it's under the bar you have to get on your knees."

Bubbles: "I'm a vegetarian, because I want to help animals go to college."

Q: Bubbles, why don't you like to travel?
A: I don't like traveling because I need to speak foreign.

Bubbles: "Remember, you always have to keep up to date, on up to date things."

Bubbles on being arrested: "I got arrested the other day. So I went to court and the Judge told me he was giving me community service. I said, Your Honor that's one of the main reasons I'm here. The Jury, and the people in the court room started laughing, and the judge got real mad. He told me he was going to slap me with contempt of court. I had to ask "How did you know I like being slapped?

Friends, these are all no shitters. You'll be amazed at what you may hear at the club or anywhere else for that matter, all you have to do is listen.

Lost Vagina

Here is another story along the lines of strip club first. As I have said many times, I've been around the world twice, seen everyone once, watched two white whales screw and a monkey fuck a football, but I've never seen or heard anything like this before...

One night I'm attempting to close up shop and walking by the dressing room when I hear giggling, screaming and high pitched voices, going on about how one of the girls had lost her vagina.

Boys and girls, this is once again one of those, "W.T.F?" moments!!!!

Of course, as you may guess, it was at this point that curiosity got the cat so to speak. This dilemma peeked my interest. At the very least, it brought up a lot of questions. First one obviously being, how does one lose a vagina? I have never heard of a stripper losing her vagina. I would think that is something that one would want to hold on to.

It's kind of counterproductive to lose the old money maker, especially in a full nude club. Could she work without it? How would I sell that?
"Come on in. The world's only beaverless stripper appearing now on stage, boys and girls she's just like a Barbie Doll!" She would break bad on the panty removal portion of the show and NOTHING!!! What a buzz kill. I can see the customers leaving the stage scratching their heads in confusion already.

Or on the other end of the spectrum, I could get the other girls to lose their vaginas too. It may solve lots of problems. No drama, no arguing, no fighting, and the constant bitching and gossip would probably go way down. We would have a lot more space in the dressing room too. Would a vagina be easier to work with than the dancer that brought it in? How would a vagina get on stage? More importantly, how would they collect the $$$Money$$$, and then where would they put it?

Maybe we could put the vaginas in little boxes with locks on them, and rent them out by the song for guys to stare at. Just charge their credit card. Now that shit would actually work. Bunch of drunken guys sitting around a table comparing vagina's like football trading cards. It could start up a whole new fad, kind of like fantasy football but better.

Yes sir. Vagina's on parade. Come on down. Get you a seat; grab a cold beer and a hot box. Squirrel curtains not included. What's the downside of this scenario? Girls would always wonder what happened to their vagina, where it's been, what did it do last night? I guess that is not really a down side. Hell, I have some girls that do that now on a nightly basis. We have to consider theft. I mean some guys get possessive over a little vagina. I have seen it happen over and over again.

Now we introduce into the scenario a small box that someone can put in their pocket and just walk out the door. That, my friend, is a serious issue. We would have to assemble a VRT (Vagina Recovery Team). What kind of specialty training would that take, how could I track them down? Who would I pick to be on a V.R.T.?

Can you imagine a female coming back to collect her vagina at the end of the evening, and then I have to explain why it's not there? That would be one pissed off bitch.

Hell that brings up a whole other issue. How would we identify each vagina and get them back to their rightful owner? Do we tag it with a little name tags, tattoos, or piercings? Some girls wouldn't mind but I know a lot more who would. I mean that would be one hell of a mix up. You can't just intermingle girl's vaginas, put them in a bag shake it around and hand them back out at the end of the evening. It's just not right.

Then, what if girls started switching vaginas? Hey, it's not out of the realm of possibility, I've listened to girls talk about their vaginas, and how other girl's vaginas look. Maybe the girls would want to trade up. Not necessarily steal another girl's vagina, but test drive it for a day or two, let the boyfriend or girlfriend take it out for a spin.

In the past, I have had girls tell me that they wished their vagina wasn't as skinny. They want a fuller, puffier style pussy. Like the ever so popular triple cheese burger model. They just think it's more esthetically pleasing. One girl even told me that she wanted a full on camel toe. My suggestion was to buy smaller pants or vacuum puff it up. She stated that she had already tried that and continued to explain to me that she could never really get that look because her vagina was small and compact.

Then you got the devious bitches that would kidnap a vagina and hold it for ransom. How much would a dancer pay to get her vagina back? The loss of one's vagina, what kind of psychological trauma would that cause? What if someone stepped on one? That would be like stepping on a banana peel. Then of course we have the legal liability of a slip and fall accident. Shit. I can imagine it now—some drunk ass customer, face down, ass up, complaining that a free range vagina got in his or her way, or under their feet and caused him to fall down.

Could a vagina survive by itself in the wild? Never mind the blunt force trauma and possibility of being tread upon by drunken revilers and pissed off girl friends. *What is the life expectancy of a vagina without its host?*

Anyway there I go rambling again.

As you can tell, I have to do something. I've got to help this poor girl find her vagina. So I go into the dressing room and calm down the natives who all were as you may have guessed extremely intoxicated and acting like giddy school girls making fun of the poor dancer who was still claiming to have lost her vagina in the first place. Add to the fact that she also is shit house wasted (I know hard to believe) and is still convinced that she is missing her vagina.

The old cop in me comes out. In order to help a person find a lost vagina you have to retrace your steps. As in any great detective story, you have to gather evidence you have to start at the beginning. So I start to question the allegedly vagina less victim. When was the last time you saw your vagina? Was it on stage, or here in the dressing room? Did someone take it from you, or did it just fall off? How do you think you lost it?

The response I received was, "I don't know. All I know is, it's just not here anymore." She then attempted to wriggle out of her skinny jeans to provide me with tangible evidence of the actual loss of her vagina.

While in motion she went ass over tea kettle and fell on the floor. Somehow she popped the top button of her pants and they came right off. She continued to drop her britches about knee level exposing one tiny little Irish vagina, perfectly positioned between her legs where God and everybody thought it should be all anatomically correct and everything. No muss, no fuss, no visible damage, no fur or fuzz, bald as a stripper's beaver should be and exactly where it was supposed to be.

Luckily as one may imagine being a dressing room for strippers there are mirrors all over the place. I picked up our little dancer and pointed out the location of her vagina. Pulled up her little pants, smacked her on the ass for good measure.

Another crisis averted

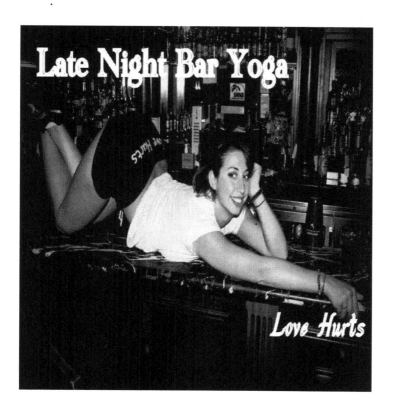

The Ranting of a Mad Stripper

While in the dressing room one day I found a diary or a diatribe of ranting from one of the girls. It could have been something from Stripper Theater or the dictated mutterings of an old sun burnt, dick whipped whore. One foot is on the stage and the other in a puddle of beer. It would seem that she was contemplating her life which looks as if it is one bad decision followed by the next and fearing mandatory retirement from the game, while attempting to exit stage left from the full contact beauty contest that had been her life as gracefully as possible.

This is a peak in the working mind of a burnt out stripper. Sit back, strap in, and hold on for this ride; Like any other bitch that perverts morality for ten hours a night in high heels, I dream of a companion waiting at the home with warm words and a hot foot bath to cure the night's disease.

So far my home greetings entail crunched toes, new blisters, and the reflection of myself swimming in a six a.m. cocktail.

I sit waiting for the next era of doom to begin. Ears still ringing and I'll greet them again with painted eyes, speaking through smeared lipstick how good it really is to be alive. It's amazing how clever and coy one can be when cornered to cover the cries. Oh but what life was…Does my greatness flicker? Oh…. My nerves are shot! Damn, that's not what I meant, damn revisions. The producers will never get that I was speaking through artistic expression! I am who I am. Call me a tool. I'm glad to be of use.

It's always a crisis around here. I weep, I fast, I pray! All I have anymore are my demons and masturbations and even those aren't too good anymore. Reflect! It is best you don't. It was my life for the job and now the job is my life. Career was not a word in my book. Of course we won't discuss the number of years that have passed by… passed on….sunk to the bottom of the glass. Doing time with jazzy drunks and lonely moons… I have measured my life in disco tunes, broken roosters and midnight rendezvous. Am I still a peach? I can't seem to keep the perfume strong enough these days.

So this fellow wondered into the establishment and said he wants Tafas. He was looking for Mediterranean. So I jumped in his lap and said, "Hey honey I'm from Greece, welcome to the show."

He asked to see a little cleavage so naturally I obliged. He handed me a dollar! So I slapped him! Like I can't keep up with the young broads! Honey, they can't even touch this elegance! Sure a dollar was worth something in my day, but fives are the new ones … Nowadays its $5 & $10's throw in a $20 and we'll call it even. You can't even get a dirty joke for fifty cents around here anymore. Keep up with the times. What's a girl got to do to get some respect around here?!

Ahh it's a recession…Everyone wants a handout…. I've certainly noticed the rations on ass! Forget about finding a good date around here! I might as well be the wall of vagina! That's too many twats for me! Let me tell you something that I learned long ago…. When they really want it, a hole in a tree will do!

Then the men come and go talking of who is next to blow. And what about love?! Roses on the vanity running around like a faggot in bloom. Of all the strip joints in the entire world he had to walk into mine.

What do you say when you meet someone, "I fondle cocks for a living, is that OK?" It's ok when you make less than what you came in with and you spend what you got on a pint of whiskey.

Mother said "If you haven't any pocket lettuce, you'll wind up eating yard food. Oh, Mother…. Humph Mother.

It was not my mother's fame that tore us apart. She met me in her red room, cigarette and drink in hand. Struggling heroically to find a connection, she certainly knew how to look like she was listening but little gushes of flattery gave her away. They landed on me like raindrops falling and haphazard, reminded me that I was invisible as ever. Yes when my mom got drunk… not sure if it was the Gin or the eau de toilette. Well she never liked the taste of my shimmer. She would tell her friends that I couldn't decide if I wanted to be an angel or a man.

Well I'm no princess, it just isn't me. But what do they know talking over tea; they're still out there where it matters!

They do not know I learned all this by watching her. Yes I am what her savage love hath made me… And I was to be her shooting star She passed it down, all the glamour.

Like ties of the sacred girdle and with my own spark of divine fire so we couldn't exactly make things Holy but we made them possible.

Well, no show is royal if the queen is wearing tears. But… how much should one endure for a cheer? We know there's a way out, we just don't care! Just go on like a dick whipped, sun burnt, old tan whore. Sunken eyes like a blood shot badger. I'm all right as long as I'm not too drunk to notice when the truth lights come on. It's hard not to notice that face of oh my god terror starring back at me! The stocking just don't fit like they used to honey.

What you really mean is you don't want to buy me a drink. You just want to fuck me extra rough. Teeth on counter of life it's like a lone slab of meat in the road.

The end.

That there was a mind trip.

Times Up

Well boys and girls I hope that everyone had a good laugh and enjoyed this read (something off of the beaten path, so to speak). I want to thank you for picking it up. If you've been to Key West, you know the deal. If you haven't and are still a skeptic, all I can say is pack your bags come on down, check it out for yourself.

and if you just happen to wonder into a Strip club Or Daddy Day care. Say Hi to the girls for me. slap a buck or two in the collection plate, garter belt or just throw it on the stage they'll pick it up

About the Author

Charles Meier is a Texan transplanted to the island of misfit toys when the U.S. Navy decided to station him here in the 1990's.

He has attempted escape this place many times but it would seem that the island wants him and the lifestyle, warm weather, cold drinks and good looking women keep him here in Key West.

While on permanent sabbatical to the island he's made the best of it. He is a casual hero that has worn a lot of hats. He's been everything from a military man to mercenary. A cop, fireman, pilot, boat captain, minister, motivational speaker and as of the writing of this misadventure, a strip club messiah. He's the true embodiment of a pirate born 200 years too late. He is an adventurer. He has crossed rivers, opened doors, rescued hostages, saved lives, explored the oceans, hunted for treasure, emptied saloons, organized orgies, satisfied the ladies and may have started a revolution or two in the process. He has been shot at and missed, shit at and hit, beaten up, blown up and stabbed (most of these on the same day). He's a brother, father, husband, son, and friend. Many have said he is a real character with character.

If you liked this book check out my other book also

Made in the USA
Charleston, SC
24 January 2017